T0099339

The Comic Strip Collection

Lucky

HI THERE. I'M PRINCESS AI OF AI-LAND. MY LIFE IS FULL OF GOOD LUCK!
EVERYONE LOVES AND ADMIRES ME.
MY BEST FRIEND LISSA IS MY HOME-SCHOOL TUTOR. HOW LUCKY IS THAT?
LISSA
YAY! YAY!
THIS WEEKEND'S MY BIRTHDAY-- WHAT LUCK!
YEAH? YOUR 13TH BIRTHDAY!
SIGH

Teen

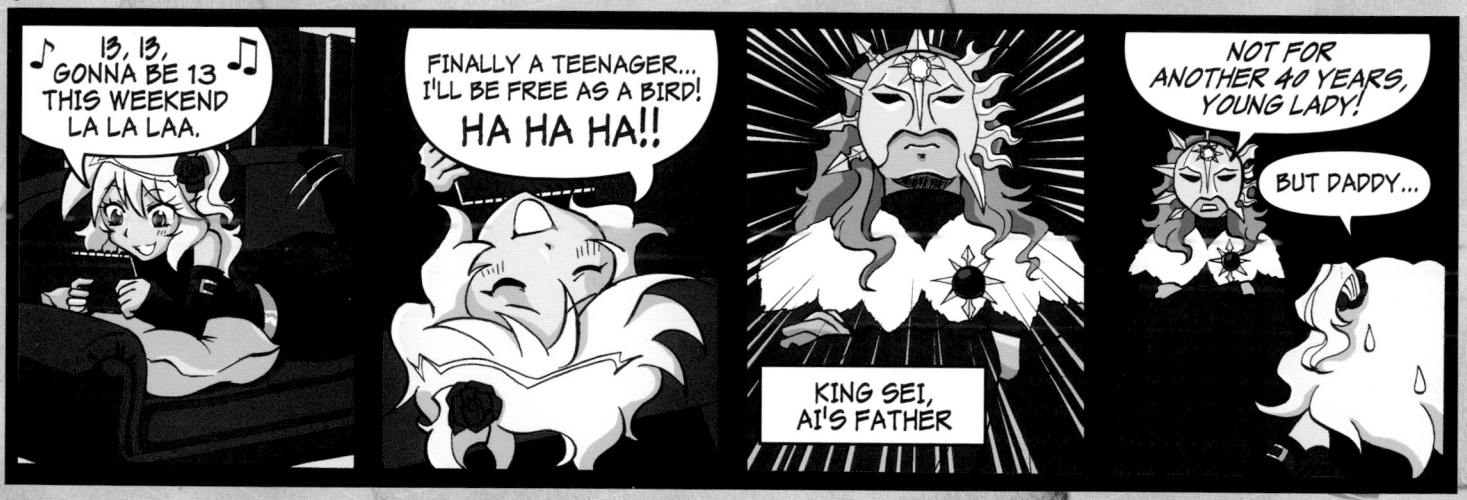
♪ 13, 13, GONNA BE 13 THIS WEEKEND LA LA LAA. ♫
FINALLY A TEENAGER... I'LL BE FREE AS A BIRD! HA HA HA!!
KING SEI, AI'S FATHER
NOT FOR ANOTHER 40 YEARS, YOUNG LADY!
BUT DADDY...

Birthday Present

Invite List

Birthday Cake

Birthday Fashion

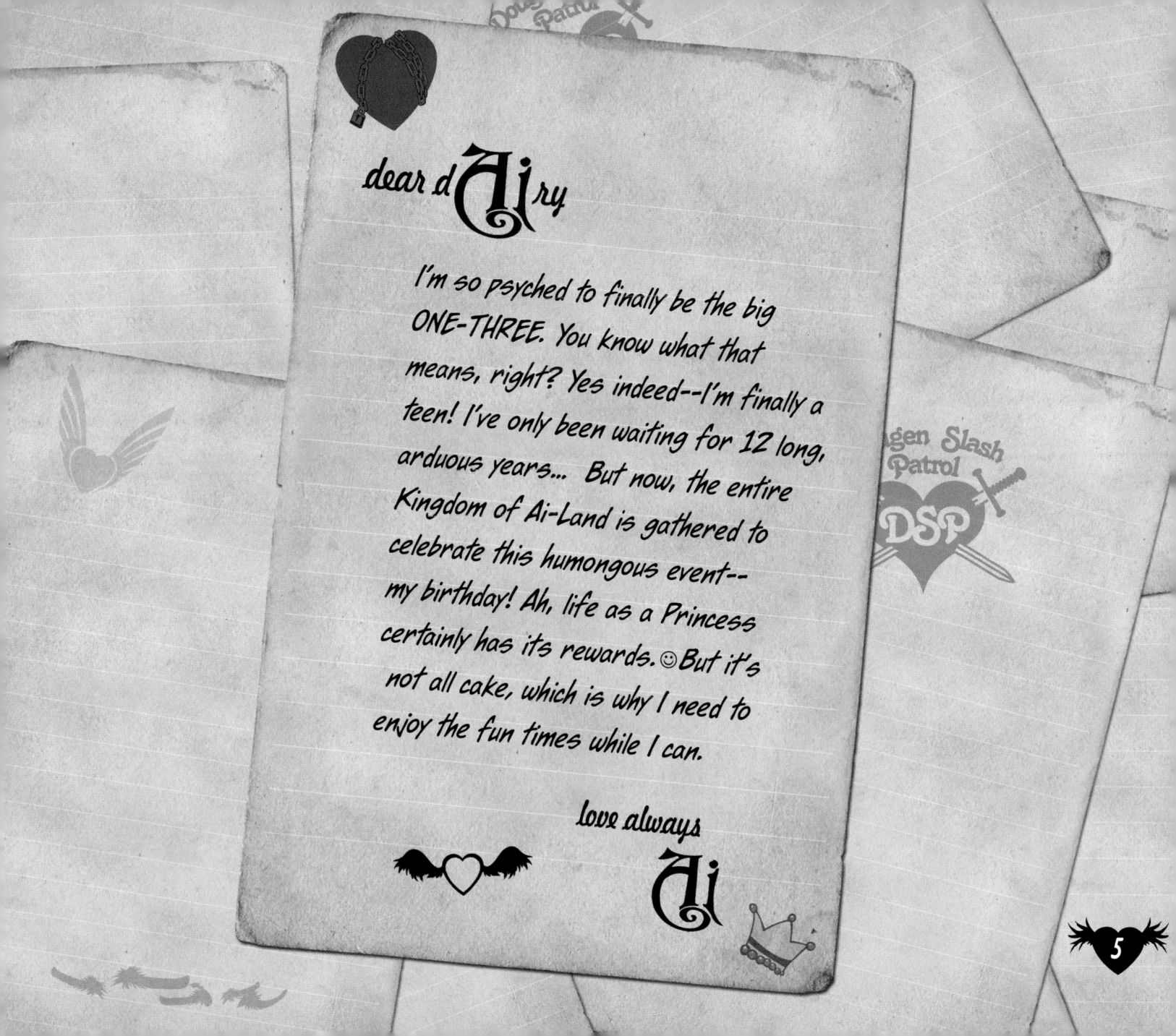

dear dAiry

I'm so psyched to finally be the big ONE-THREE. You know what that means, right? Yes indeed--I'm finally a teen! I've only been waiting for 12 long, arduous years... But now, the entire Kingdom of Ai-Land is gathered to celebrate this humongous event--my birthday! Ah, life as a Princess certainly has its rewards. ☺ But it's not all cake, which is why I need to enjoy the fun times while I can.

love always

Ai

HAPPY BIRTHDAY, PRINCESS AI!
YOU LOOK RADIANT!
YOU REPRESENT OUR ENTIRE WORLD'S HOPES AND DREAMS!
THANKS-- YOU'RE ALL SO KIND!
MY GIFT TO YOU, AI.
OMIGAWD IT'S HUGE! THANKS DADDY.
IS THAT A BULLDOG-BIRD?
!!
IS THE KING FEELING WELL?
LOOKS SCARY...
A BABY DOUGEN.

MANY BREEDS OF DOUGEN ONCE DOMINATED AI-LAND. NOW THEY ARE ALMOST EXTINCT.
BUT THIS RARE BREED IS KNOWN TO BE CANTANKEROUS, SO BE CAREFUL WITH HIM.
HI, LITTLE GUY! DON'T MESS WITH PRINCESS AI, OKAY?
HE'S SOOOO CUTE!
YUCK.
I THINK HE *LIKES* YOU.

Pet Food

Nocturnal

Pet Shots

Pet Clothes

Walk

NICE CHOICE-- THE GOTHIC ONE.
READY FOR YOUR FIRST WALK?
Yank!
NOW, BE A GOOD BOY...
HEEEEY!
WAIT FOR MEEEE!
WONDER WHO'S WALKING WHOM?

Bath

QUIT SQUIRMING IF YOU DON'T WANT SOAP IN YOUR EYES!
SOAP
HEY, STOP IT! HA HA HA! I'M NOT HA HA HA KIDDING!
PRINCESS, IS EVERY-THING OKAY IN TH--
YOU TWO ARE HAVING WAY TOO MUCH FUN.

dear dAiry

Life here in the Ai-Land castle is good, especially now that I've got my fun-loving, rascal baby-Dougen pet to entertain Lissa and me. I hear that Dougen are a special breed of living beings here on Ai-Land, but they are almost entirely extinct. That's why I'm so glad Daddy gave me one for my 13th birthday! I guess it helps that he's the King. Now if I can only find a way to train this little guy...

love always

Ai

WHAT A WEEK IT'S BEEN, HUH, LITTLE GUY?
RRRRLLLP!
RAWK!
YOU'RE GONNA NEED TO CALL HIM SOMETHING BESIDES "LITTLE GUY."
LIKE REX OR FIDO OR...
IF ONLY WE CAN FIND A NAME THAT FITS HIS PERSONALITY...
raucous;
Rau•cous (adj).
Rowdy, disorderly.
English-Enochian Dictionary

Dougen Slash Patrol
DSP

Other Side

Nations

Religion

Ai-Land vs. the Other Side

Transportation

Bad for You

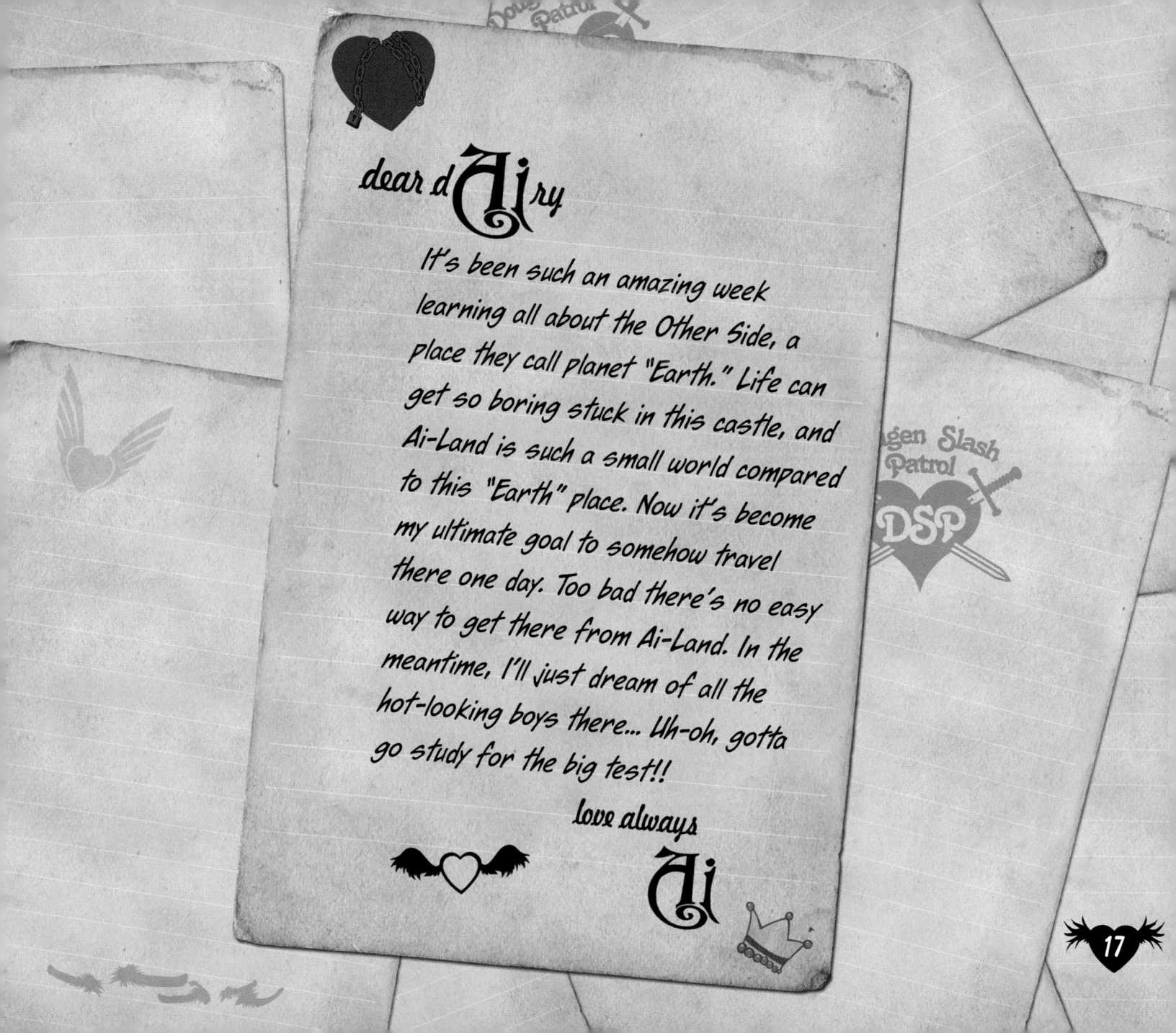

dear dAiry

It's been such an amazing week learning all about the Other Side, a place they call planet "Earth." Life can get so boring stuck in this castle, and Ai-Land is such a small world compared to this "Earth" place. Now it's become my ultimate goal to somehow travel there one day. Too bad there's no easy way to get there from Ai-Land. In the meantime, I'll just dream of all the hot-looking boys there... Uh-oh, gotta go study for the big test!!

love always

Ai

THIS IS YOUR BIG EXAM BASED ON YOUR STUDIES THIS WEEK ABOUT THE OTHER SIDE, PLANET EARTH.
FIRST QUESTION: WHICH MODE OF TRANSPORTATION IS THE FASTEST?
Q5: NAME THREE FORMS OF MONEY.
Q6: WHICH RELIGION BELIEVES IN NIRVANA?
Q7: IN WHICH COUNTRY IS PARIS LOCATED?
EASY STUFF!
ALL DONE!
PRINCESS, ARE YOU SURE YOU ANSWERED EVERYTHING?
YUP, EASY AS PIE!
ALL CORRECT.

Dougen Slash Patrol
DSP

Wings

Can't Fly

Secret

King Sei

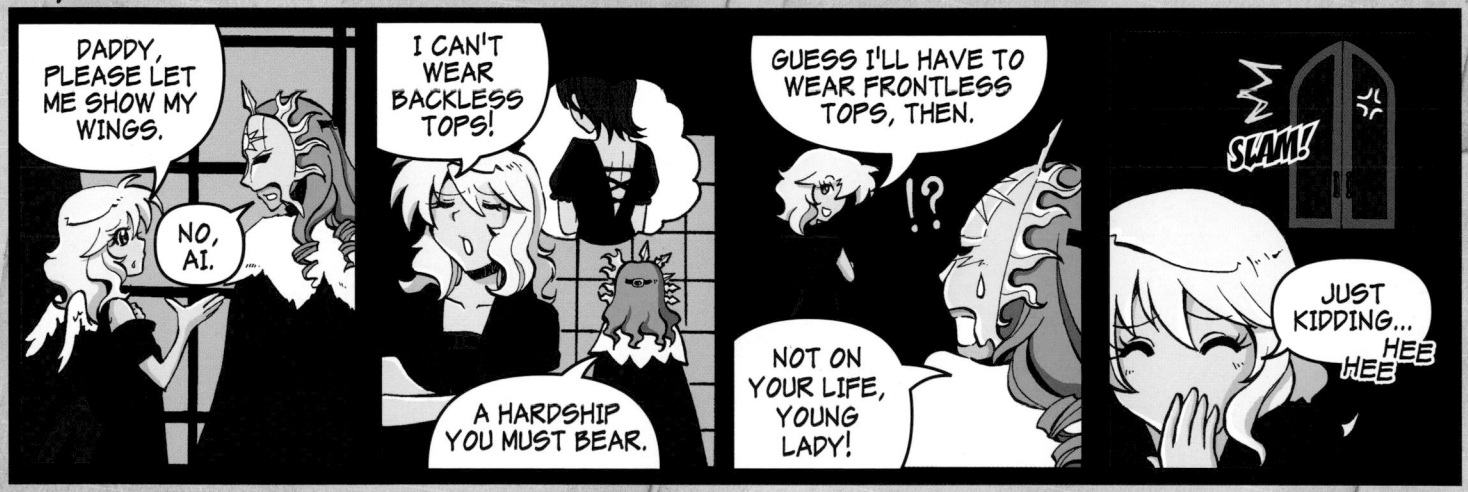

Practice Flying

Cosplay

dear dAiry

Life as the sole Princess of Ai-Land is so full of trials and tribulations. Sure, the shopping sprees are fun, but why am I the only human stuck with wings? I feel like a freak! Worse yet, Daddy insists I never reveal them to another soul--not even my best friend and tutor Lissa. So hopefully my little "fake wings" scheme will work...

love always

Ai

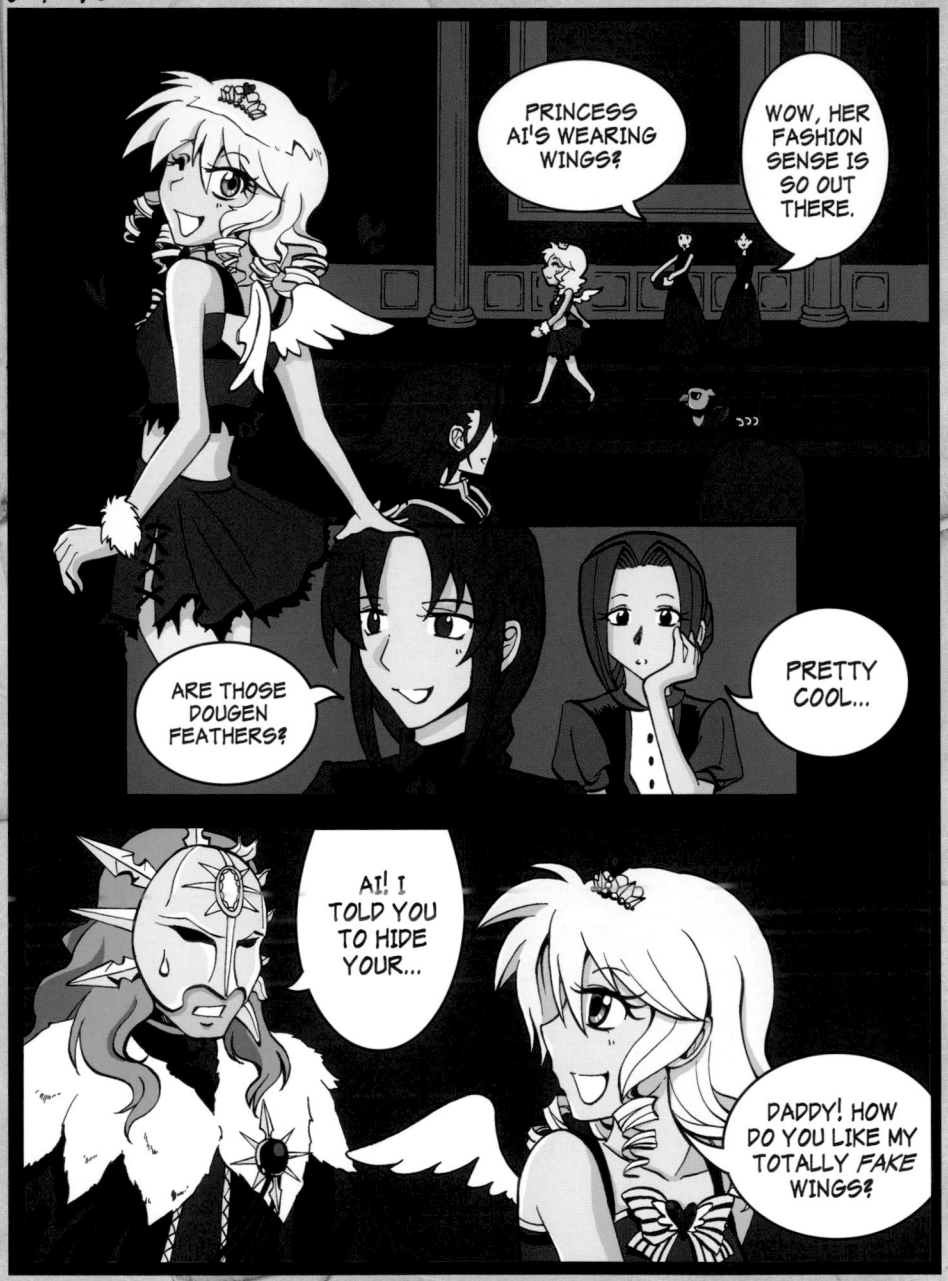
PRINCESS AI'S WEARING WINGS?
WOW, HER FASHION SENSE IS SO OUT THERE.
ARE THOSE DOUGEN FEATHERS?
PRETTY COOL...
AI! I TOLD YOU TO HIDE YOUR...
DADDY! HOW DO YOU LIKE MY TOTALLY *FAKE* WINGS?

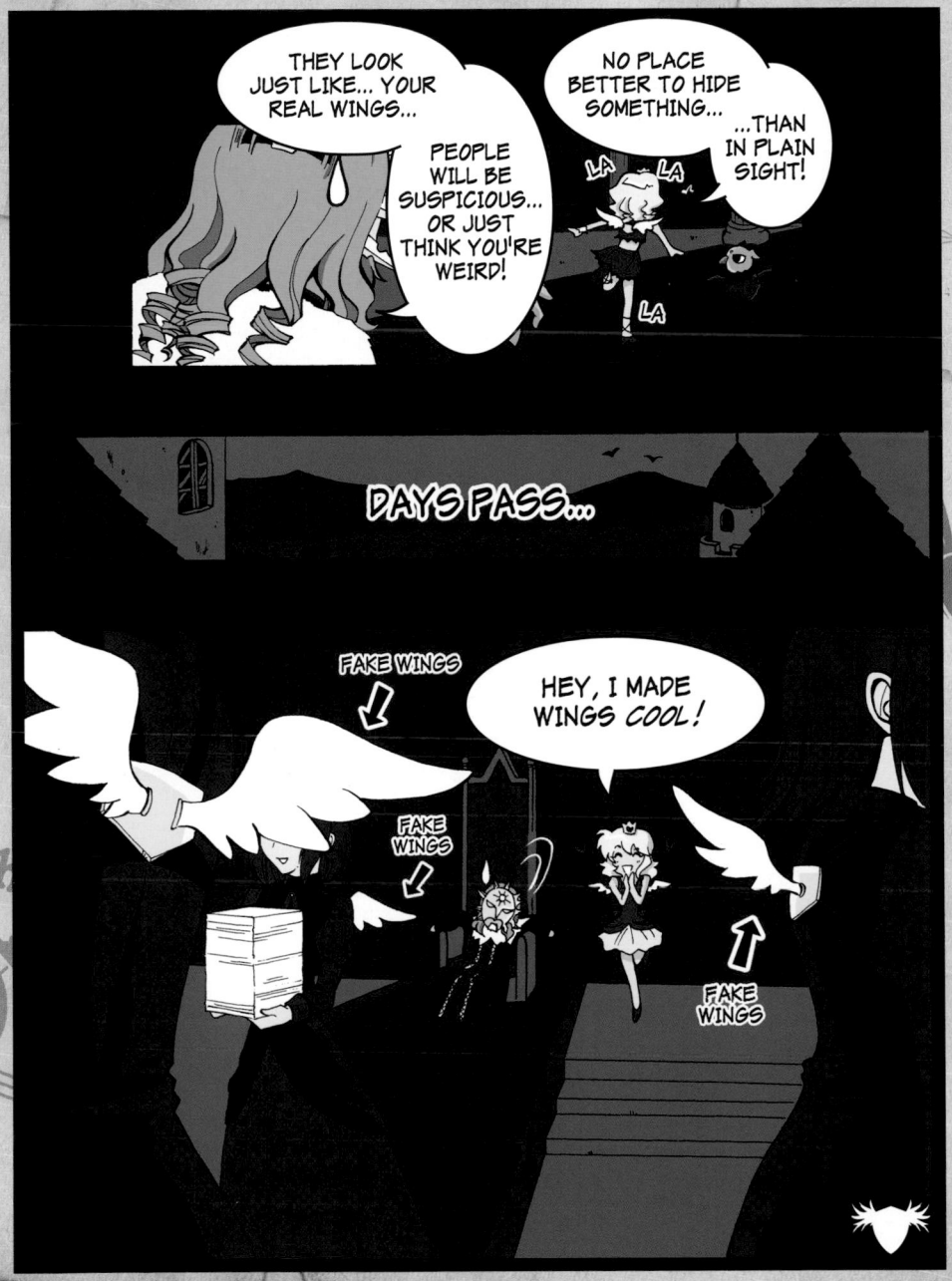

Dougen Slash Patrol DSP

Not a Princess?!

Adopted?

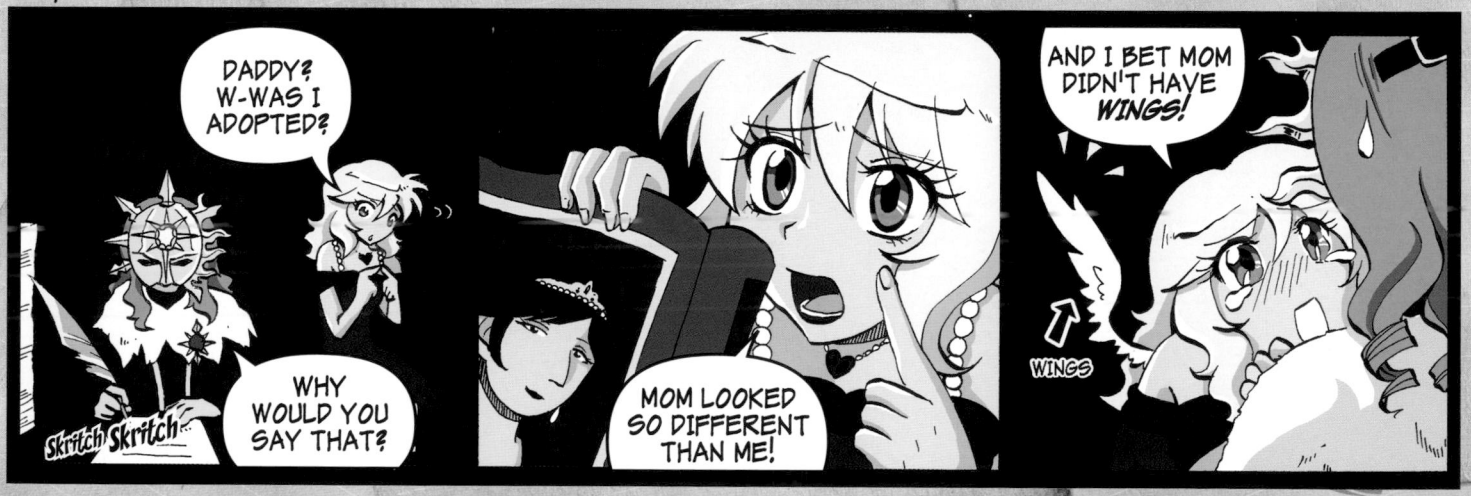

Fatherly Love

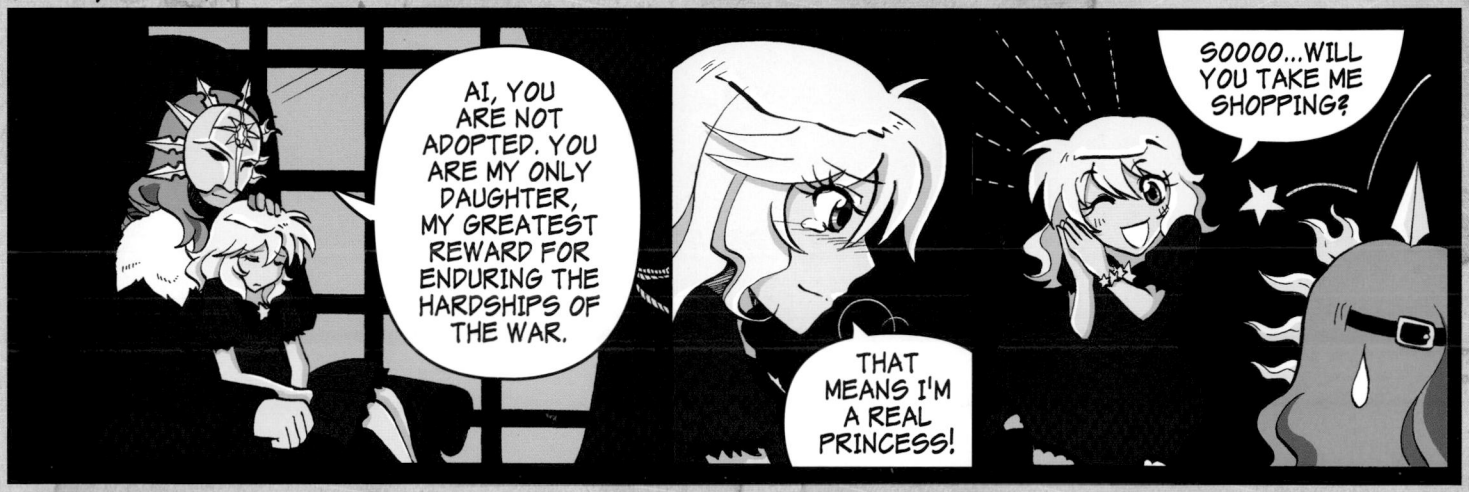

Evil Ruler

Dating

Dad's Job

dear dAiry

Ai-Land is a special place, and I'm lucky to be Princess, but sometimes I feel so different than everyone else. My dad's not only a king, but he always wears a mask. Mom died as I was born--so I never even saw her. And of course, there are my wings--No human has wings! I can't help but wonder who I really am...

love always

Ai

AI, YOU'RE EVEN MORE BEAUTIFUL THAN YOUR MOTHER WAS.
I WISH I'D KNOWN HER. WHAT WAS MOM LIKE, DADDY?
CHARMING
BEAUTIFUL
CHARISMATIC

INTELLIGENT... PERHAPS EVEN A BIT CONNIVING... BUT A TRUE ANGEL.
SHE SOUNDS JUST LIKE ME!
NOT EXACTLY, MY DEAR...
WHEN SHE WAS YOUR AGE, SHE DID ALL HER HOMEWORK, WENT TO BED ON TIME AND ATE HER VEGETABLES.

Fashion Mags

Lissa's Outfit

In the Mall

Shopping Break

Shoes

HOW ABOUT *THESE* SHOES, PRINCESS?
WE'VE BEEN THROUGH EVERY SHOE IN THE SHOP.
SOCK DEPT.
Tired...
EXCEPT THIS ONE...
AGGG!
SIGH...
COOL SOCKS, GOT ANY MORE?

Guys

OOOOH, LISSA, LET'S "ACCIDENTALLY" BUMP INTO THOSE HOT PUNKBOYS!
HERE THEY COME...
BUMP!
WHOOPS!
PLEASE FORGIVE ME, PRINCESS!
Flomp!
THAT'S NO BOY!
OH, NO!

dear dAiry

Shopping is by far the best perk I get for being Princess of Ai-Land. Of course, Daddy rarely lets me leave the castle. He's way too overprotective, even though I'm already 13. But every now and then I get my way.

love always

Ai

WE'RE HO-O-O-OME!
WELCOME BACK, YOUNG LADIES. I TRUST YOU ENJOYED YOURSELVES?
YES, DADDY. THANKS FOR LETTING US GO SHOPPING.

AND YET... I SEE YOU CARRY NO BAGS? YOU WINDOW-SHOPPED ONLY?
I MARVEL AT YOUR SELF-DISCIPLINE, YOUNG LADY!
UH, YOUR MAJESTY...
AHEM... IT SEEMS I SPOKE TOO SOON.

Homework

Studying

Music & Arts

History

Sleeping Beauty

Report Due

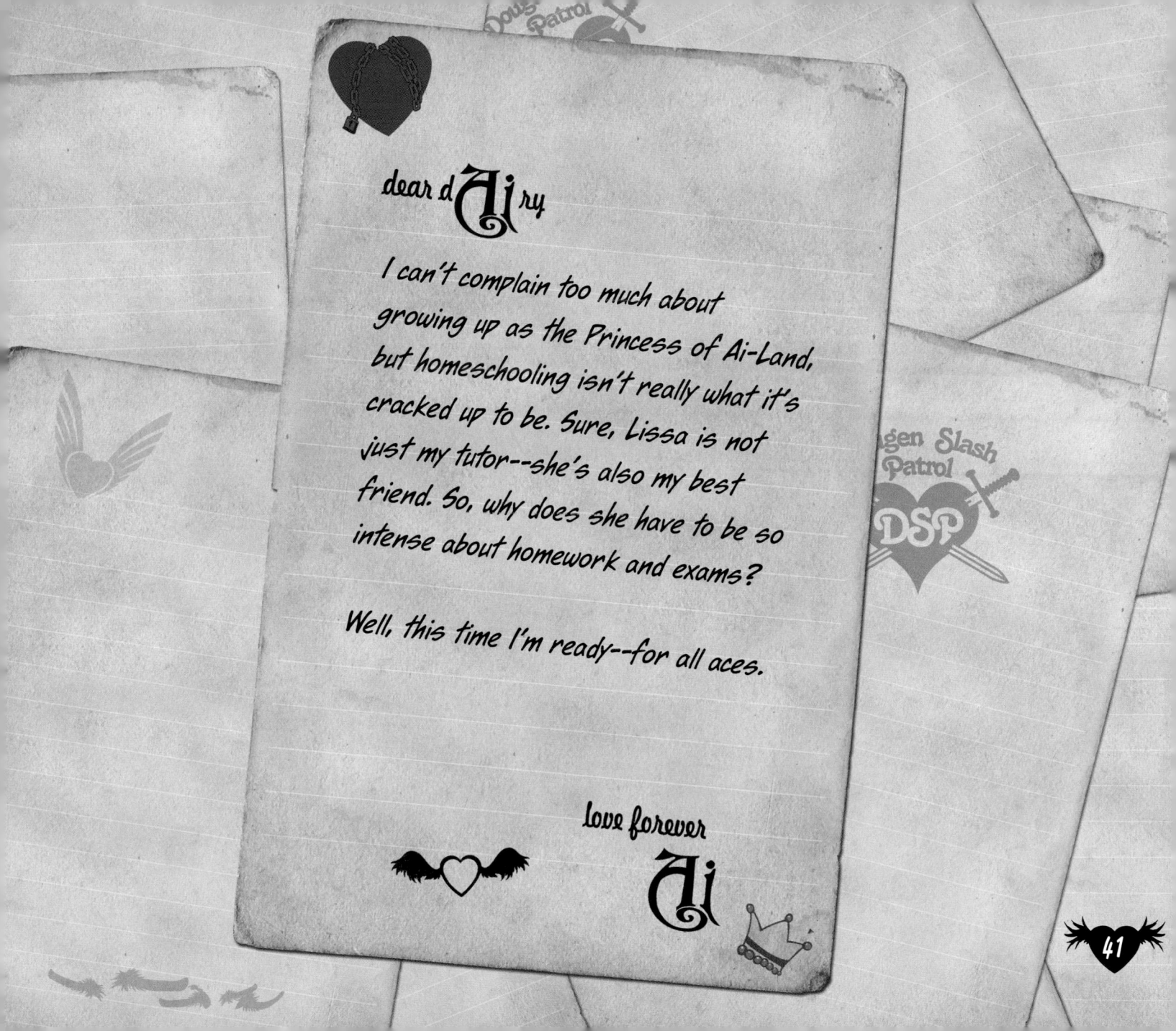

dear dAiry

I can't complain too much about growing up as the Princess of Ai-Land, but homeschooling isn't really what it's cracked up to be. Sure, Lissa is not just my tutor--she's also my best friend. So, why does she have to be so intense about homework and exams?

Well, this time I'm ready--for all aces.

love forever

Ai

FIRST MIDTERM EXAM OF THE DAY, PRINCESS. IT'S TWO HOURS, SO PACE YOURSELF-- YOU'LL HAVE TWO MORE TODAY AND THREE TOMORROW.
02h 00m 00s
I'M READY TO KICK EXAM BUTT!
READY... SET... GO!

Dougen Slash Patrol DSP

Tickets

Together

Results

Reward

We're Going!

Suspicious

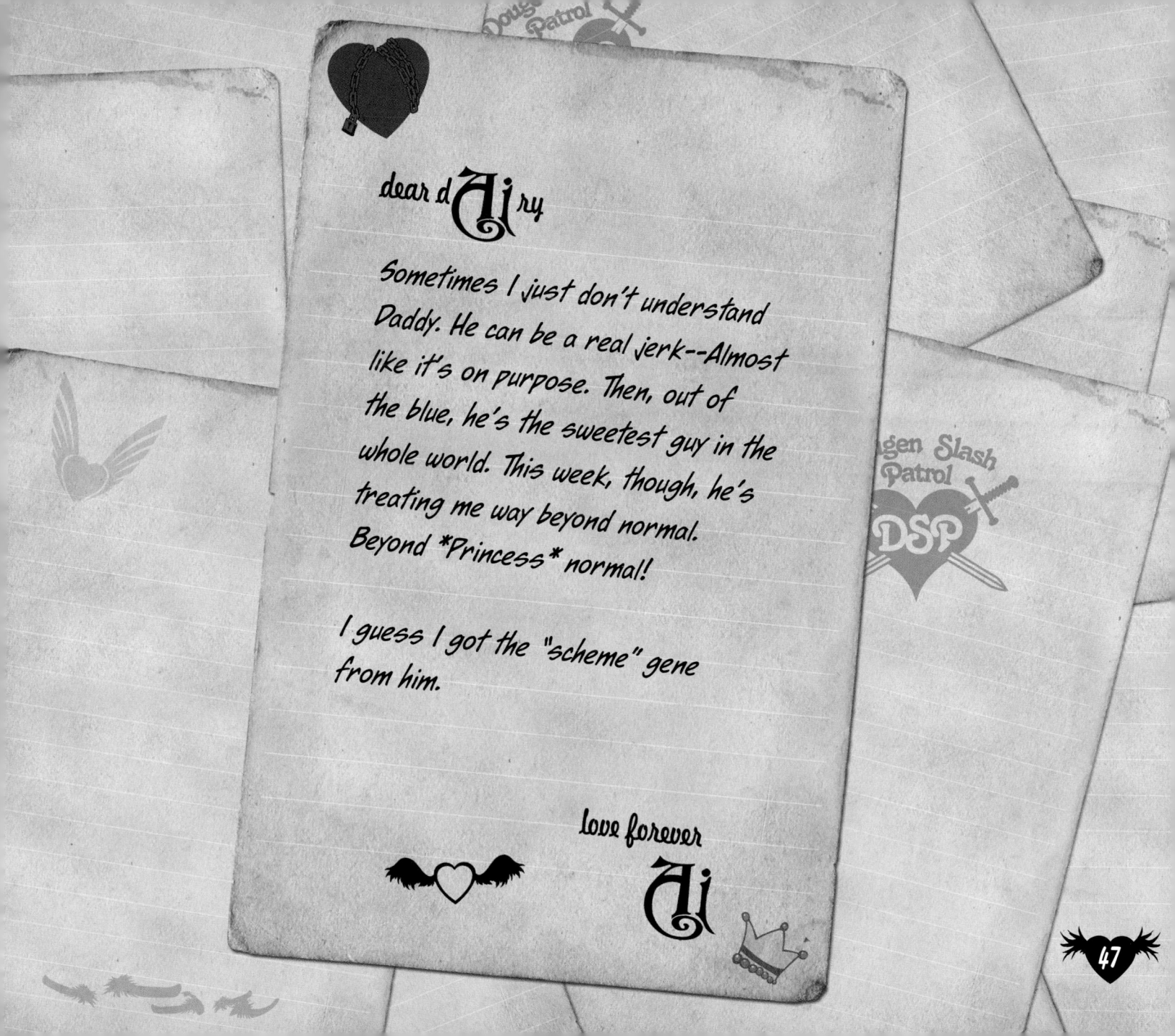

dear diary

Sometimes I just don't understand Daddy. He can be a real jerk--Almost like it's on purpose. Then, out of the blue, he's the sweetest guy in the whole world. This week, though, he's treating me way beyond normal. Beyond *Princess* normal!

I guess I got the "scheme" gene from him.

love forever

Ai

FIRST, THE CONCERT TICKETS, THEN YOUR SUSPICIOUSLY NICE BEHAVIOR, NOW THIS HUGE FEAST--
I CAN'T TAKE IT ANY MORE! DADDY, WHAT ARE YOU SCHEMING?
HONEY, I JUST WANT TO REWARD YOU FOR ACING YOUR EXAM.
COME ON, DADDY. WHAT DO YOU REALLY WANT?
SIGH
AI, YOU KNOW ME TOO WELL...

THE TRUTH IS... NEXT WEEK IS THE AI-LAND DEBUTANTE BALL. YOU'RE FINALLY THIRTEEN--
NO WAY!
YOU WANT ME TO BE FRILLY, PRIM AND PROPER? FORGET IT!
NOT EVEN IF I GIVE YOU BACKSTAGE PASSES TO THE DOUGEN SLASH PATROL CONCERT?
PASS
Backstage?
YOU JUST GOT YOURSELF A DEAL.
BAN

Concert Plans

Concert Outfits

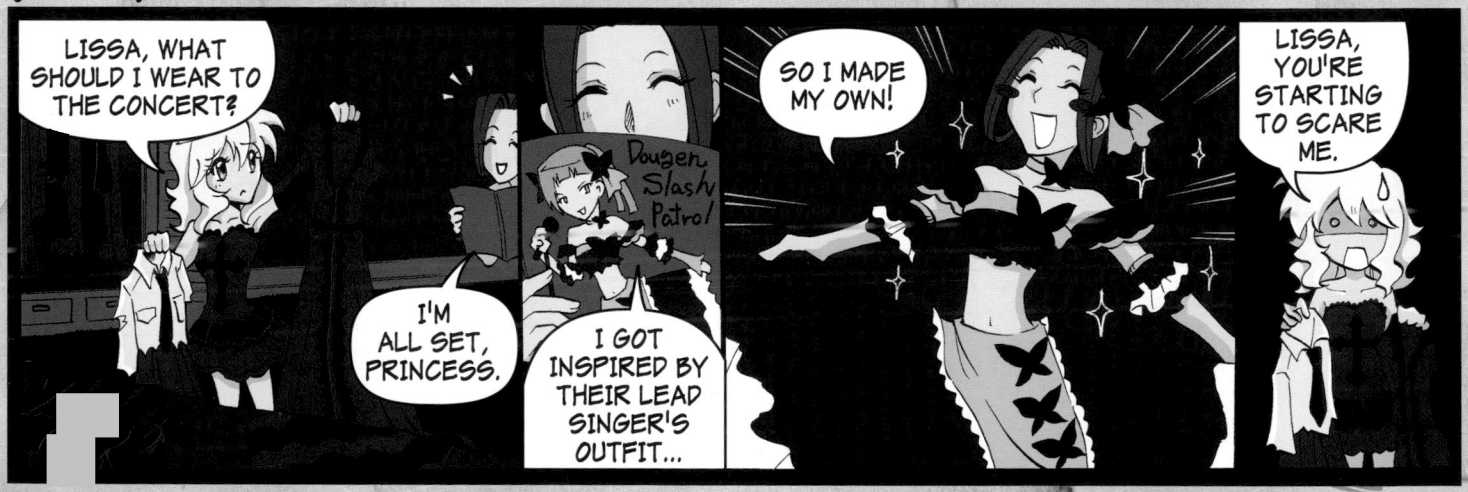

Concert Night

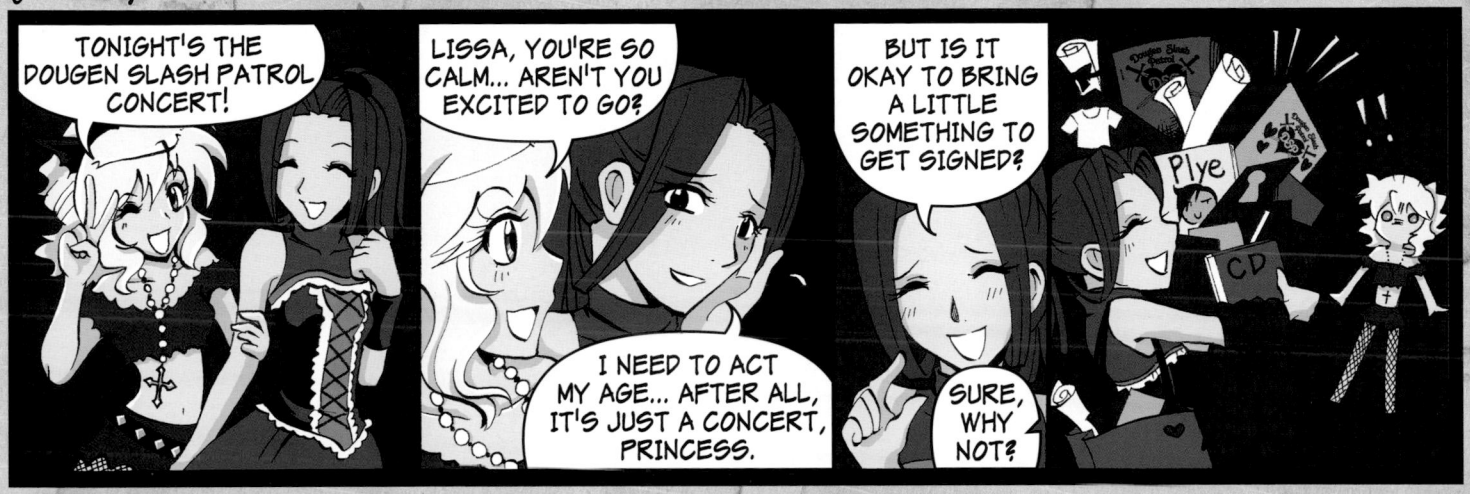

Groupie on a Rampage

After the Show

Backstage

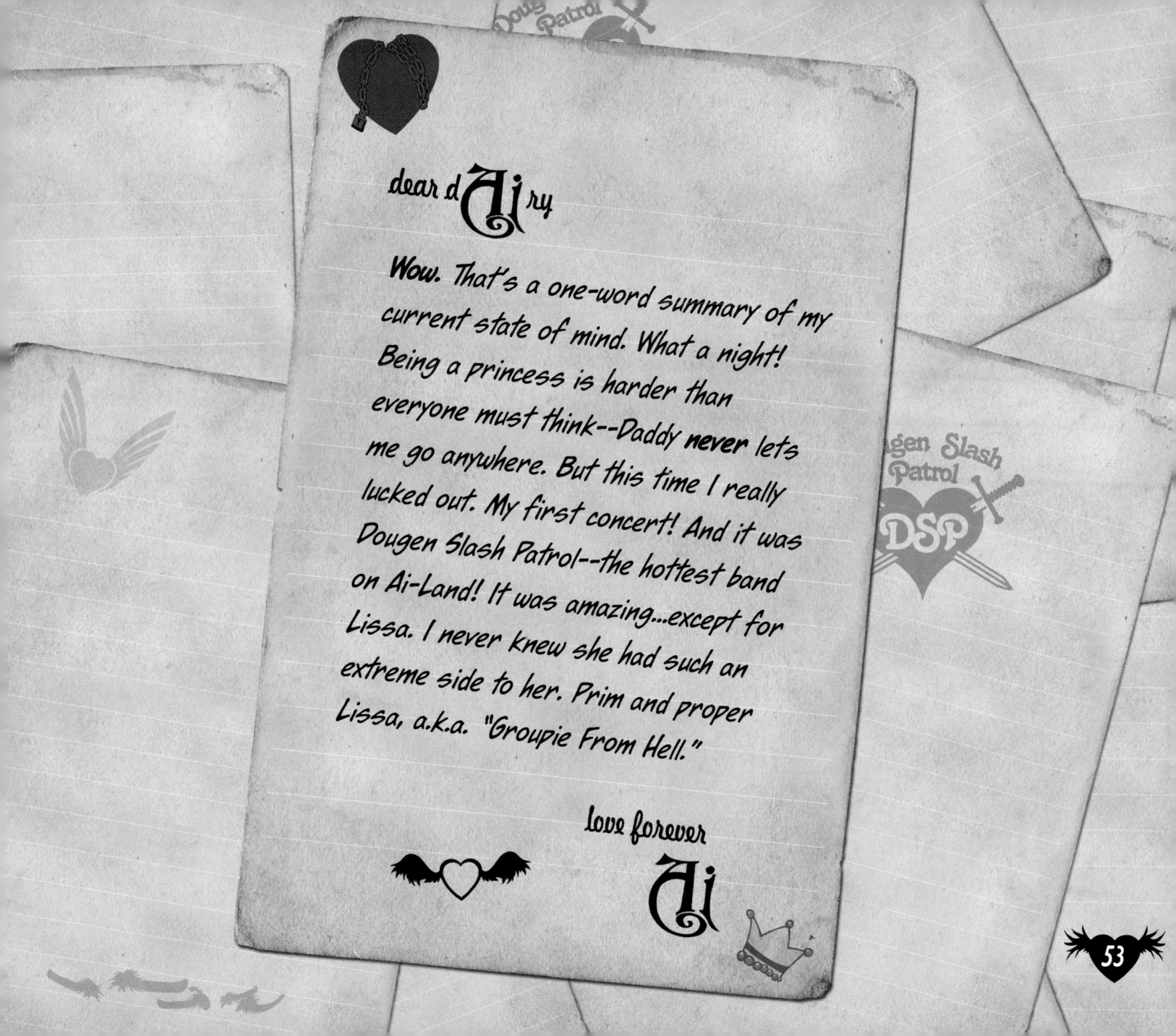

dear diary

Wow. That's a one-word summary of my current state of mind. What a night! Being a princess is harder than everyone must think--Daddy **never** lets me go anywhere. But this time I really lucked out. My first concert! And it was Dougen Slash Patrol--the hottest band on Ai-Land! It was amazing...except for Lissa. I never knew she had such an extreme side to her. Prim and proper Lissa, a.k.a. "Groupie From Hell."

love forever

Ai

DOUGEN SLASH PATROL WAS ABSOLUTELY THE BEST CONCERT EVER--I CAN'T BELIEVE I GOT PLYE'S AUTOGRAPH!!
LISSA, YOU GOT ENOUGH SWAG TO LAST THE NEXT FEW CENTURIES.
OFFICIAL GUIDE BOOK
CD
I KNOW I GOT OUT OF HAND AT THE CONCERT. THANKS SO MUCH FOR UNDERSTANDING ME, PRINCESS.

YOU KNOW, I'M *YOUR* NUMBER ONE FAN, TOO.
IT'S GREAT TO SEE YOU SO PASSIONATE ABOUT SOMETHING YOU LOVE.
SQUEEZE
I FORGIVE YOU, LISSA.
BUT YOU BETTER NOT CALL ME A VAMP AGAIN...
BACK OFF, YOU VAMP!
HISSSSSS

Luv for Music

King's Request

Debutante

Ai's Plan

Ai Style

Guitar

dear diary

Honestly, I love Lissa. She's my tutor, my best friend. Really, she's like my big sis. If it weren't for her, I'd be the loneliest girl on the planet. I guess that's why I feel so guilty for getting close to Plye. It was never about hurting Lissa. Does that make me selfish, though? I'm not sure what's right and what's wrong...

love forever

Ai

I CAN'T BELIEVE YOU GOT PLYE FROM DOUGEN SLASH PATROL TO TEACH YOU GUITAR-- IT'S NOT FAIR!!
YOU VAMP!
♪ RAZOR SHARP CUT TO MY HEART, OUR LOVE BLEEDS US APART ♪
PLEASE TAKE HER AWAY...
BEFORE SHE COMMITS AN ACT OF VIOLENCE.
YOU'RE PICKING THIS UP SO FAST, PRINCESS AI. IN NO TIME YOU'LL BE PLAYING D.S.P. SONGS BETTER THAN WE DO.
HEE HEE THANKS!

Dougen Slash Patrol DSP

Lounging Around

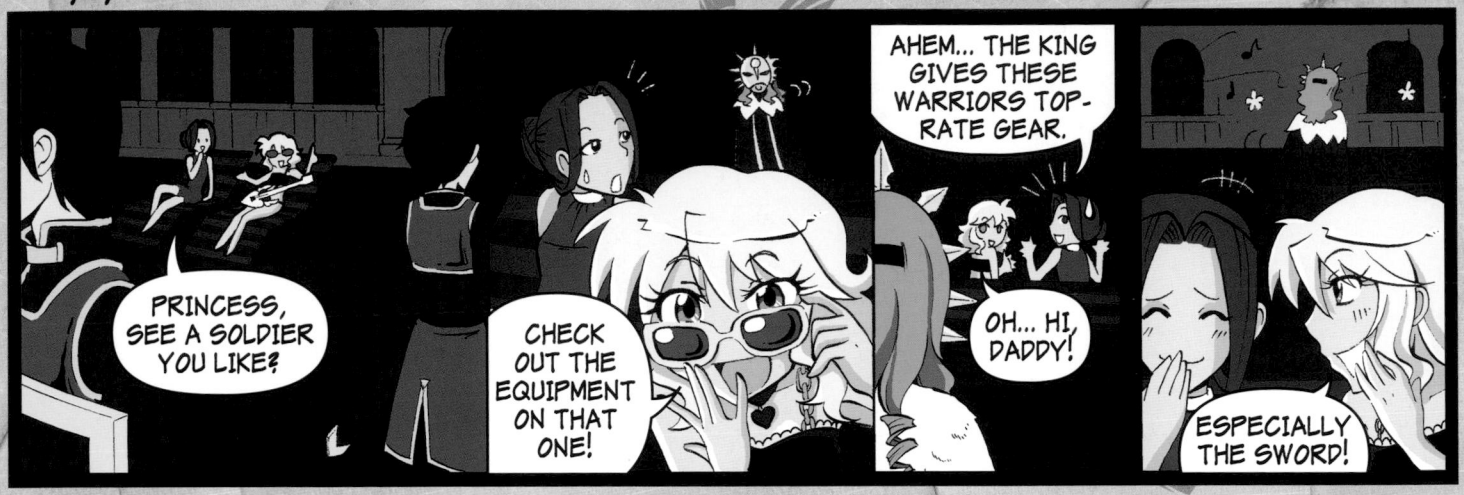

Too Serious

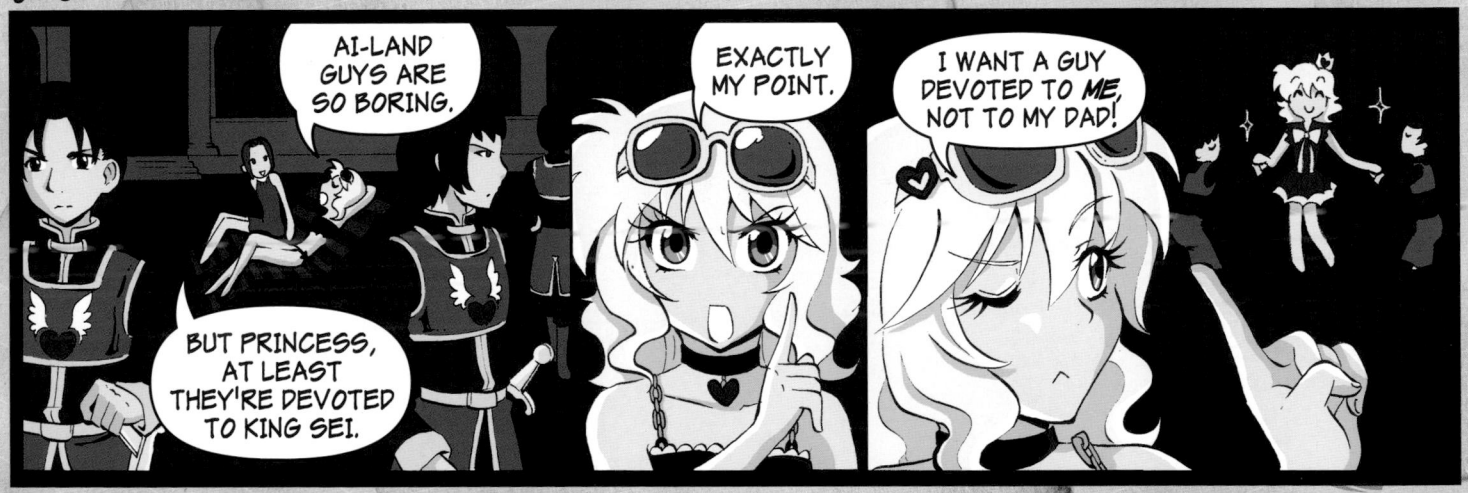

Damsels in Distress

Playin' Guitar

Cards

More Cards

dear diary

Daddy insists I'm too young to date. I think he wants me to die a virgin. Either that or he wants to choose. Well, no way Jose! I know it's part of my job as a teenager (now that I'm officially one!) to learn about guys. But one thing I'm learning about my "big sis" Lissa--she may act prude but no one loves guys more than her.

love forever

Ai

ALL THESE GUYS NOTICE MY GUITAR PLAYING...
SO WHY DON'T THEY COME OVER?
BECAUSE YOU'RE THE PRINCESS--THEY'RE INTIMIDATED.
SIGH
GUESS I HAVE TO PLAY DAMSEL-IN-DISTRESS.
PSSST! RAWK, PLAY DEAD!
RAWK!!
FLOP
OH, NO!
SOMEONE HELP THE PRINCESS!

MAY WE HELP, YOUR HIGHNESS?
IT'S RAWK, MY PET DOUGEN. I THINK HE'S...SICK. WHAT SHOULD I DO?
WE'LL TAKE HIM TO THE NURSE IMMEDIATELY, YOUR HIGHNESS!
WHAT ABOUT ME...?
I THOUGHT YOU SAID DAMSEL-IN-DISTRESS, NOT DOUGEN-IN-DISTRESS.

What a Pain

No Breaking Promises

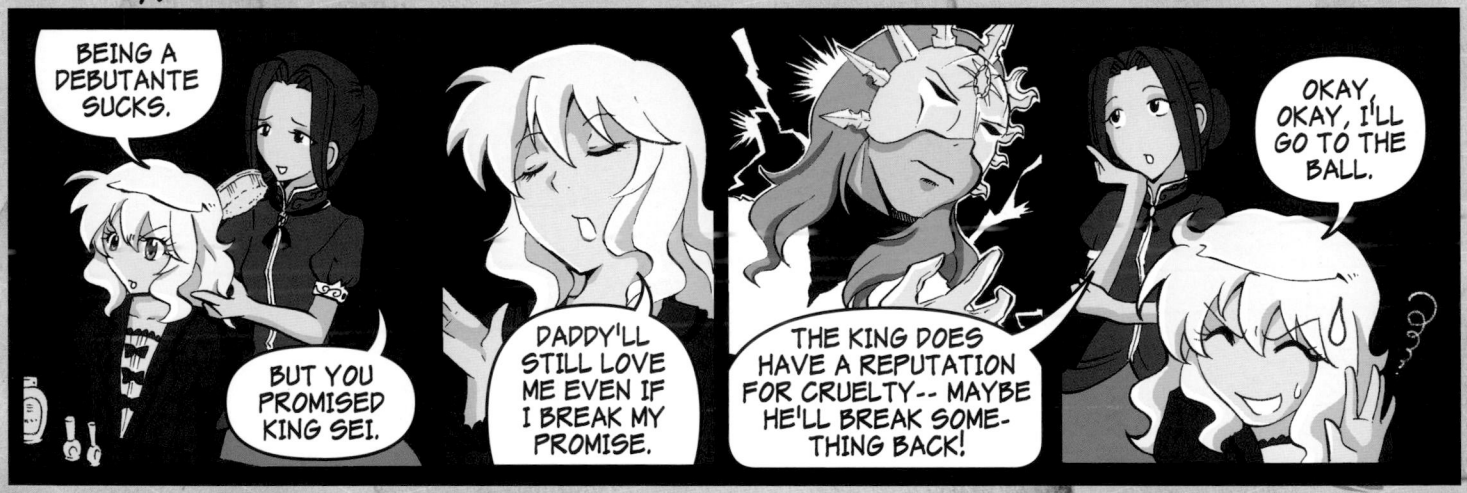

Cut Down to Size

Hot Guys

Escort Patrol

Debu-Taunt

dear diary

What is it about me that drives me to rebel? I can't help myself--all I want to do is shock everyone, especially Daddy. Am I mental? It's just so fun to see people's faces when I'm not the Princess they expect me to be (or want me to be). I can't help it, though--the more I'm supposed to act good, the more I want to be bad.

Poor Daddy.

love forever

Ai

LADIES AND GENTLEMEN...
THE DEBUTANTE YOU HAVE ALL BEEN WAITING FOR...
PRINCESS AI!!
STRUM
PRINCESS OF PAIN DARK CLOUDS POISON RAIN
FROM MIDNIGHT TO DAWN NIGHTMARES AND BEYOND
WELCOME TO THE TORTURED HEART OF THE DEBU-TAUNT!
Ai

PRINCESS, I LOVE YOU!!!!
AI!
WOO-HOO!
AWESOME!
AMAZING SHOW!
WOW!
THE KING!
UH-OH.
HERE COMES DADDY-- I BET HE HATED IT.
STOMP STOMP
YOU ARE AMAZINGLY TALENTED, AI. YOU MADE ME PROUD.
DADDY, YOU ACTUALLY *LIKED* MY DEBUTAUNTING?!

Drinks From the Other Side

Two to Tango

Stepping

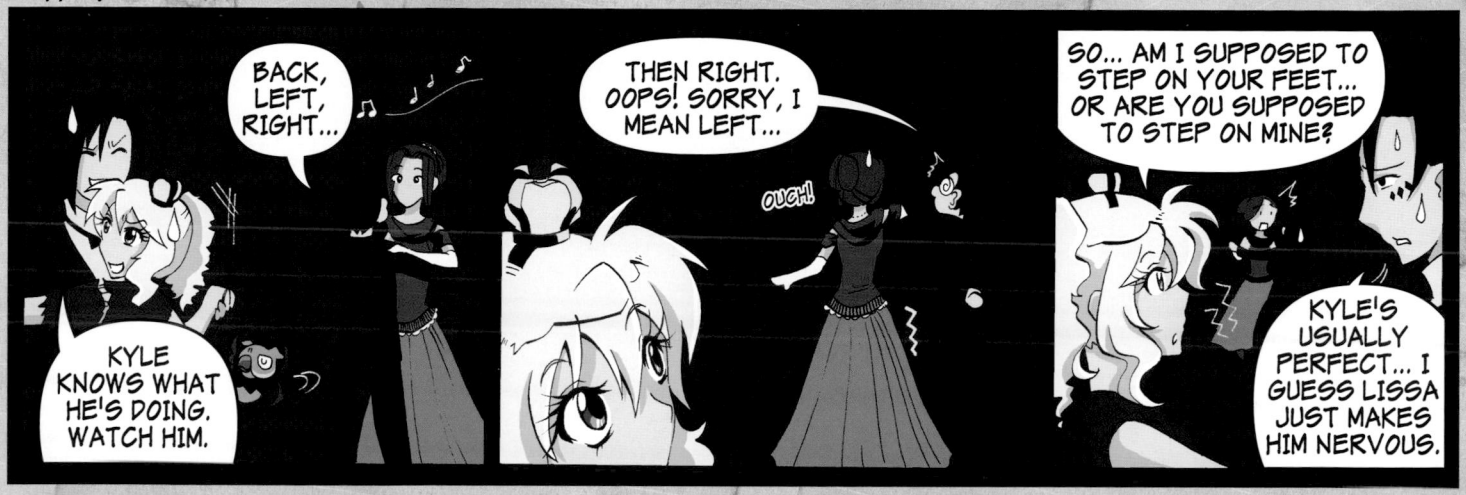

Chaperone

Full Moon

Trying Out For Size

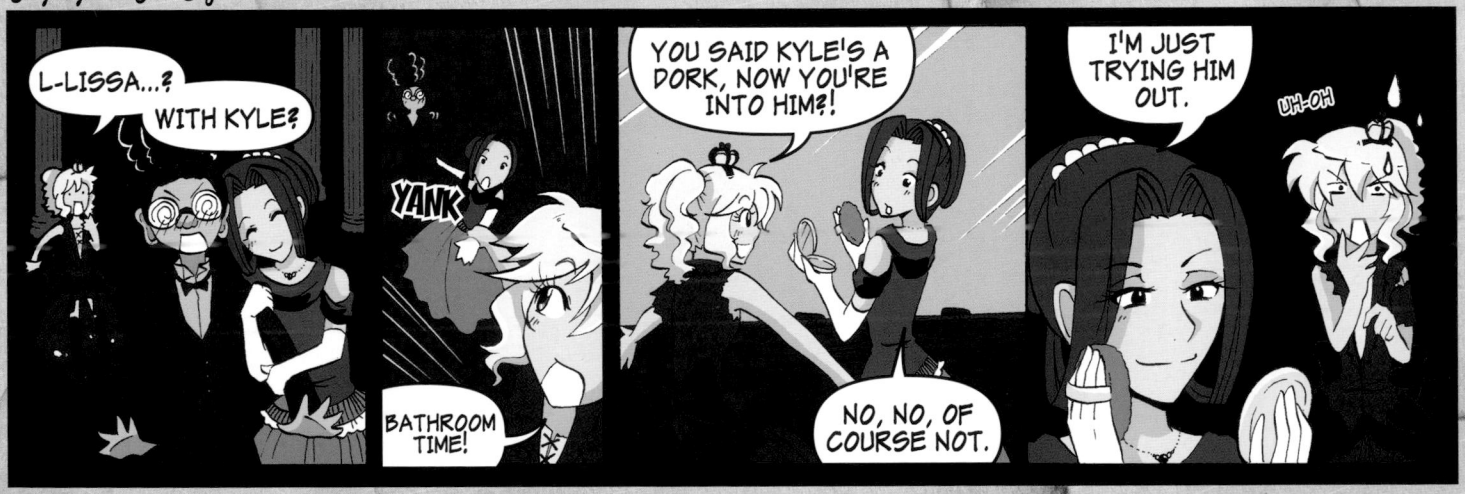

dear dAiry

Ai-Land is such a bizarre place. I wish I lived on Earth, the Other Side.

There, I wouldn't have to worry about these so-called traditions. I never wanted to be a debutante. It's just not me. But, to be honest, tonight wasn't so bad. The other girls were really cool--and even Daddy loosened up a bit and had a good time!

love forever

Ai

WHAT A CUTE OUTFIT!
I CAN'T BELIEVE WE'RE DEBUTANTES!
YOURS IS WAY MORE ADORABLE.
BUT NONE OF US CAN EVEN TOUCH PRINCESS AI.
HEY, GUYS! I GOT SOME COOL NEW HAIR BEADS FOR EVERYONE.
THEY'RE FAB!
PRINCESS, WE'RE SO PROUD TO BE DEBUTANTES WITH YOU.

Dougen Slash Patrol
DSP

Wrong About Everything

Jealousy

Guilt Part 1

Change the World

Give Back

Volunteer

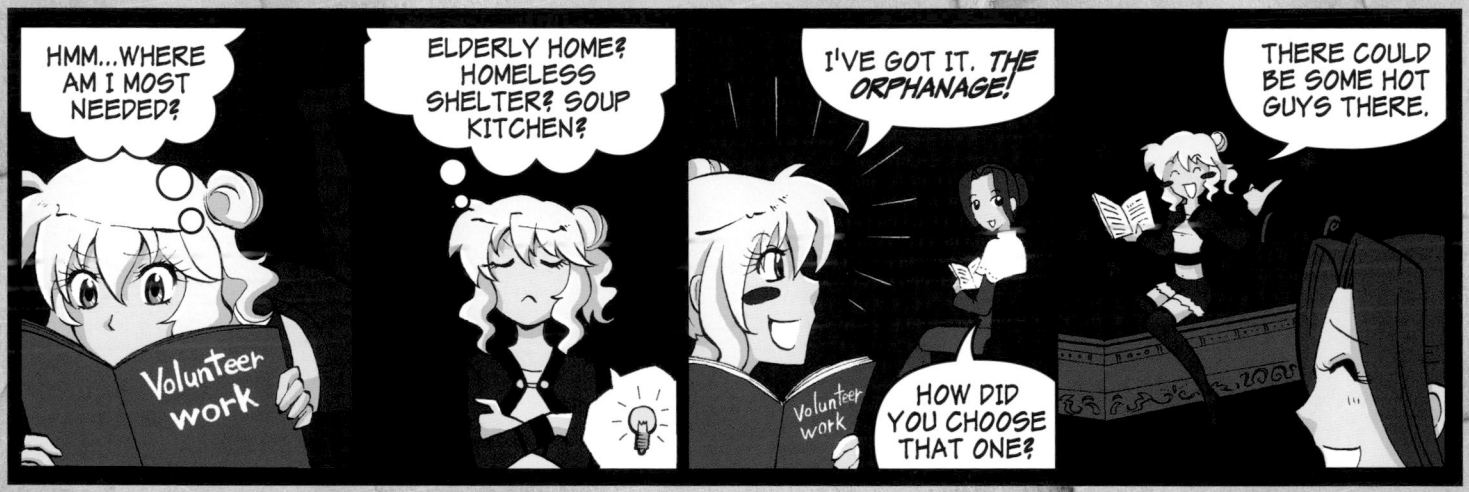

dear dAiry

I'm excited and nervous about today. It's my first time really venturing out into the "real world" of Ai-Land. As a volunteer at the orphanage, I'll get to give back to the community. Will they accept me? Will they hate me like they seem to hate Daddy? After all...I didn't ask to be born a princess. All I know is that I care about helping out. There's a voice inside of me that won't shut up--it says, "You're not who you think you are!" What if I was born an orphan? Life is fate. But we're all in this together, and I'm 13--old enough to do my share, even if Daddy doesn't like it!

love forever

Ai

WOW, PRINCESS, I'M SO PROUD THAT YOU DECIDED TO VOLUNTEER AT AN ORPHANAGE!
THANKS, LISSA.
YOUNG LADY, YOU'RE A PRINCESS. YOU DON'T NEED TO LOWER YOURSELF LIKE THIS.
SEE YA!
DADDY, BEING A PRINCESS IS ABOUT SERVING AI-LAND-- NOT ABOUT ME.
At the Orphanage
THROW IT OVER HERE!
I KNOW--LET'S USE THE HAMMER!
SIS, I MADE A BOO-BOO.
EVERYONE, PLAY TIME IS OVER.

ENOUGH ALREADY! GET TO YOUR CHORES.
HELLO...?
WELCOME, PRINCESS. I STILL CAN'T BELIEVE YOU'RE GOING TO VOLUNTEER HERE.
ARE YOU SURE YOU KNOW WHAT YOU'RE GETTING YOURSELF INTO?
I'M READY FOR ANYTHING!
GRRR!
HEY!
YAAAAHH!
ANYTHING?
UH-OH.

No Pool?

Introductions

Each Has Their Story

Veggies

Clothes

Cooking

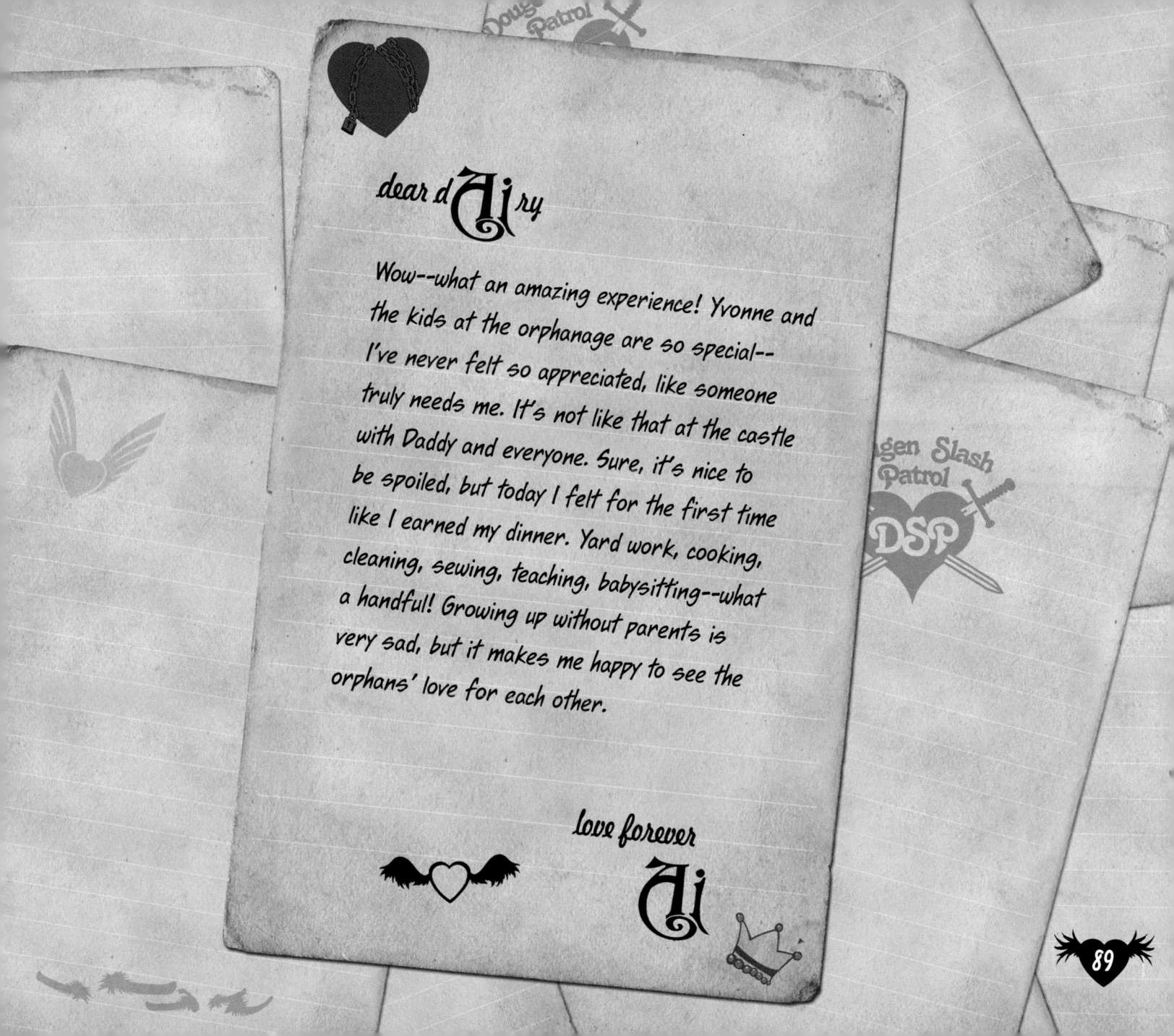

dear diary

Wow--what an amazing experience! Yvonne and the kids at the orphanage are so special--I've never felt so appreciated, like someone truly needs me. It's not like that at the castle with Daddy and everyone. Sure, it's nice to be spoiled, but today I felt for the first time like I earned my dinner. Yard work, cooking, cleaning, sewing, teaching, babysitting--what a handful! Growing up without parents is very sad, but it makes me happy to see the orphans' love for each other.

love forever

Ai

ALL RIGHT, EVERYONE! DINNER'S READY.
THAT...WOULD BE UN-SEEMLY, MAJESTY.
MY GUARDS, PLEASE JOIN US.
AS YOUR PRINCESS, I INSIST!
THANK YOU, PRINCESS AI!
WE AT THE ORPHANAGE ARE INDEBTED TO YOU FOR YOUR VOLUNTEER SERVICE.
I'VE LEARNED A GREAT LESSON HERE. YOU MAY HAVE LITTLE MONEY, BUT YOU HAVE TONS OF LOVE.
SOB SOB

THANKS FOR LETTING ME BECOME PART OF YOUR FAMILY.
NOW THAT DINNER IS OVER, IT'S TIME FOR ME TO GO.
A KISS GOOD-BYE?
NUH-UH!
PRINCESS, YOU FORGOT SOMETHING!
WHAT IS IT, THEN?
YOUR TURN TO DO THE DISHES!

Kids Running Around

Hungry?

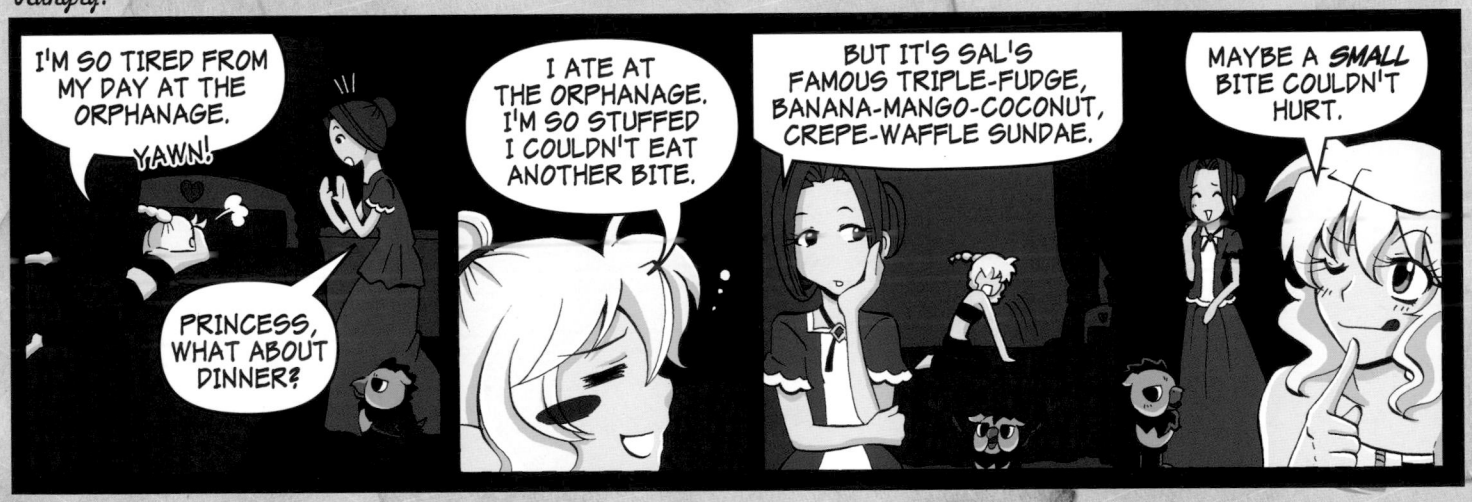

Grease

Lucky Friendships

No One Compares

Rawk & the Sundae

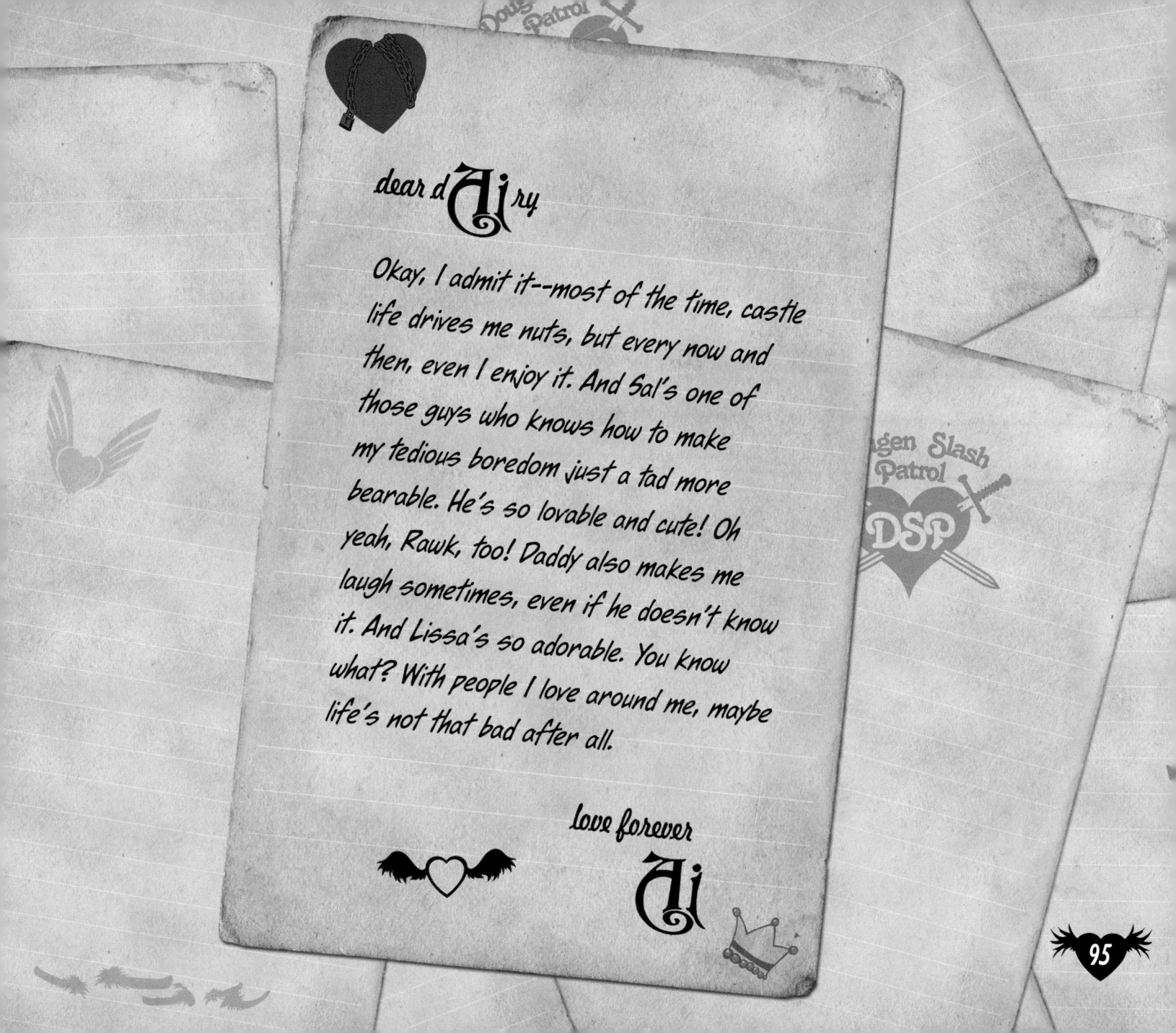

dear diary

Okay, I admit it--most of the time, castle life drives me nuts, but every now and then, even I enjoy it. And Sal's one of those guys who knows how to make my tedious boredom just a tad more bearable. He's so lovable and cute! Oh yeah, Rawk, too! Daddy also makes me laugh sometimes, even if he doesn't know it. And Lissa's so adorable. You know what? With people I love around me, maybe life's not that bad after all.

love forever

Ai

WHAT A MEAL!
RAWK CAN'T EVEN MOVE.
I CAN'T BELIEVE WE ATE A WHOLE TRIPLE-FUDGE, BANANA-MANGO-COCONUT, CREPE-WAFFLE SUNDAE!
mmmm!
HELLO, ALL. SAL, I'M READY FOR YOUR FAMOUS TRIPLE-FUDGE, BANANA-MANGO-COCONUT, CREPE-WAFFLE SUNDAE.
burp!
I'VE BEEN LOOKING FORWARD TO IT ALL DAY!
UH, MAJESTY...I ALREADY SERVED IT TO THE GIRLS AND...RAWK.
WHAT?!
BAM!
YOU DISPLEASE ME, SAL.

JUST KIDDING, YOUR HIGHNESS. I MADE A SPECIAL, ROYAL DESSERT PLATE FOR YOU!
IT'S HUGE!
THANK YOU, SAL! NOTHING CAN SPOIL MY GOOD MOOD NOW.
RRRAAWK!
yum!
mm!!
gobble!
CHOMP!
EXCEPT THAT.

Fall

Show-Off

Scary Squirrel

Axe to Grind

Mushrooms

Turtleneck

dear diary

There's something about autumn--the brisk air on my face, the brown, red and orange leaves on the trees and ground--something in the air feels both sad and exciting. It's a nice time to get outside and go for a walk. Summer's over, which of course is a bummer, but maybe this next year, something exciting will finally happen. Even though castle life can be sooo boring, Lissa and I always scheme up some sort of trouble.

love forever

Ai

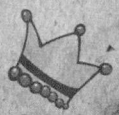

THE SOLDIERS ARE SO STRONG--LOOK AT THEM GO!
giggle
TOO BAD I SUCK AT SPORTS.
MAN! WHAT A KICK!
I'LL STICK WITH FASHION.
WATCH OUT, PRINCESS!
HUH?

OWW!
BONK!
?!
dribble
KAPOW!
HERE'S YOUR BALL BACK.
YOU SAID YOU WERE NO GOOD AT SPORTS!
I'M NOT.
EVERY TIME I TRY TO KICK THE BALL HARD, IT ALWAYS ENDS UP IN THAT STUPID NET.

Cut my Dress

Hello-ween

Pumpkins

Thick or Thin

Outfits

Costumes

dear dAiry

There's something about the Other Side--the place they call Earth--that seems so amazing. I keep thinking about it. It's my dream to visit one day. Here on Ai-Land, my life feels like it's controlled entirely by Daddy. That's why volunteering at the orphanage was so important to me. Somewhere, somehow, I feel that I can make a difference. Maybe bringing a little bit of Earth to Ai-Land can be my first step.

love forever

Ai

HAPPY HALLOWEEN
OKAY, EVERYONE, LET'S TRY THIS SPECIAL CUSTOM THEY HAVE ON EARTH.
REMEMBER WHAT I TAUGHT YOU AT THE ORPHANAGE?
Yay!
YES, PRINCESS. WE'LL TRY.
Ding-a-Ling
DON'T BE NERVOUS-- THIS'LL BE FUN!
HELLO?
WHO'S THERE?

TRICK OR TREAT!!
MONSTERS!
yikes
AND STAY OUT!
SLAM
OH, YEAH, THIS IS AI-LAND. GUESS THEY'VE NEVER HEARD OF HALLOWEEN.

Aches and Pains

Buzzzzz

Dying Cows

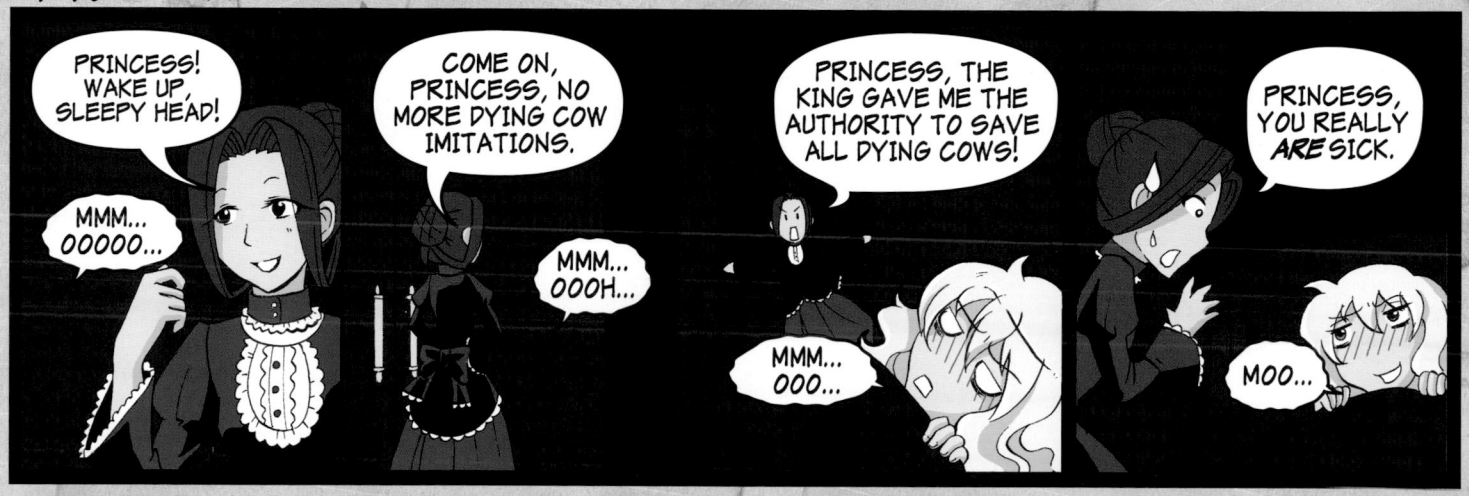

Really Sick

Say Ahhh

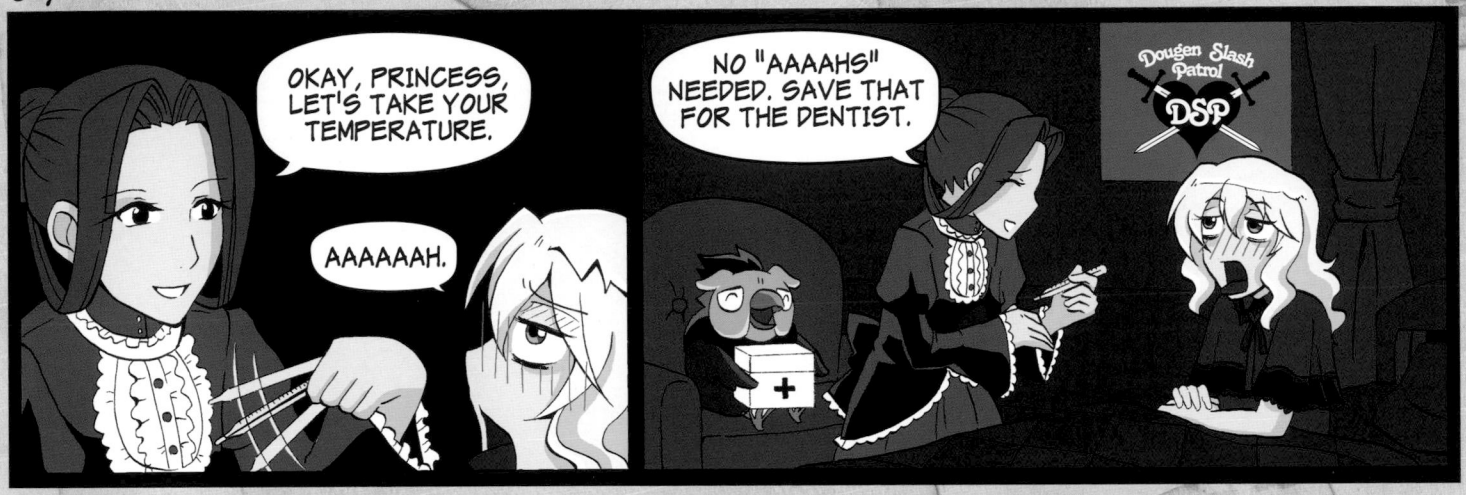

Stuck in Bed

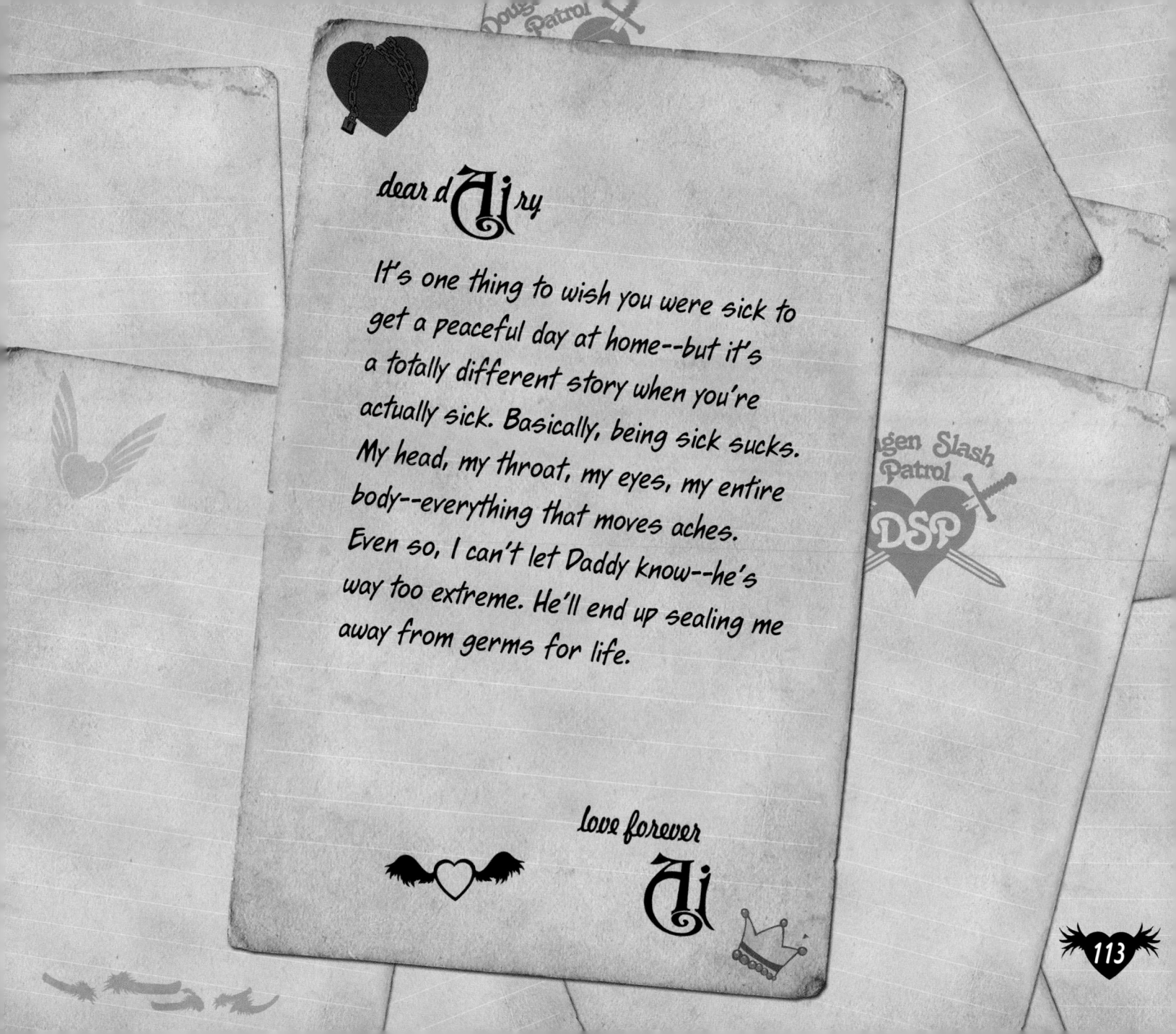

dear diary

It's one thing to wish you were sick to get a peaceful day at home--but it's a totally different story when you're actually sick. Basically, being sick sucks. My head, my throat, my eyes, my entire body--everything that moves aches. Even so, I can't let Daddy know--he's way too extreme. He'll end up sealing me away from germs for life.

love forever

Ai

PRINCESS, YOU'VE GOT A FEVER. IT'S MY DUTY TO TELL KING SEI.
OH NO. DADDY'S SUCH A WORRY-WART.
SNIF SNIF
GOOD MORNING, LADIES!
GOOD MORNING DADDY.
COUGH COUGH
AI, YOU LOOK DEATHLY ILL.
MY PRECIOUS DAUGHTER! SUMMON DOC SVENSEN AT ONCE!
DADDY, IT'S NO BIG DEAL. DOC SVENSON WILL JUST SAY, "GET PLENTY OF FLUIDS AND REST."
NONSENSE! DOC SVENSON WOULD NEVER DARE TREAD SO LIGHTLY!

DOC SVENSEN IS BRINGING ALL HIS EQUIPMENT.
WELL, PRINCESS AI, AFTER ANALYZING ALL 50 TEST RESULTS, IT SEEMS YOU HAVE...THE FLU.
BE SURE TO GET PLENTY OF FLUIDS AND REST.
SEE...

Chicken Soup

Shot of Whiskey

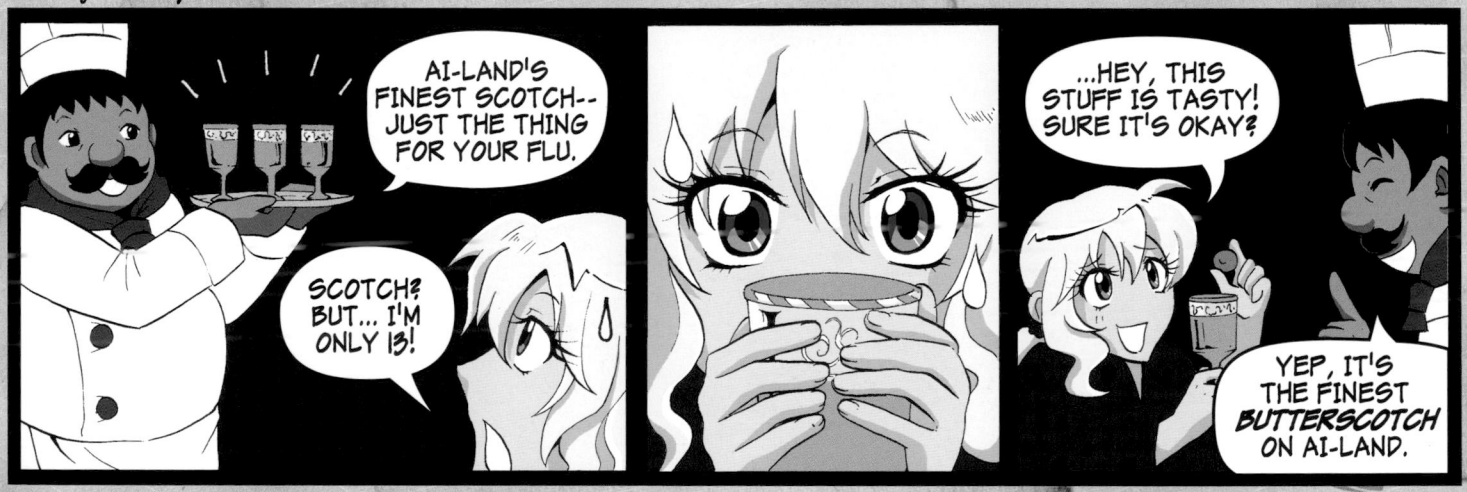

Gargle

Vitamins

Jello & Ice Cream

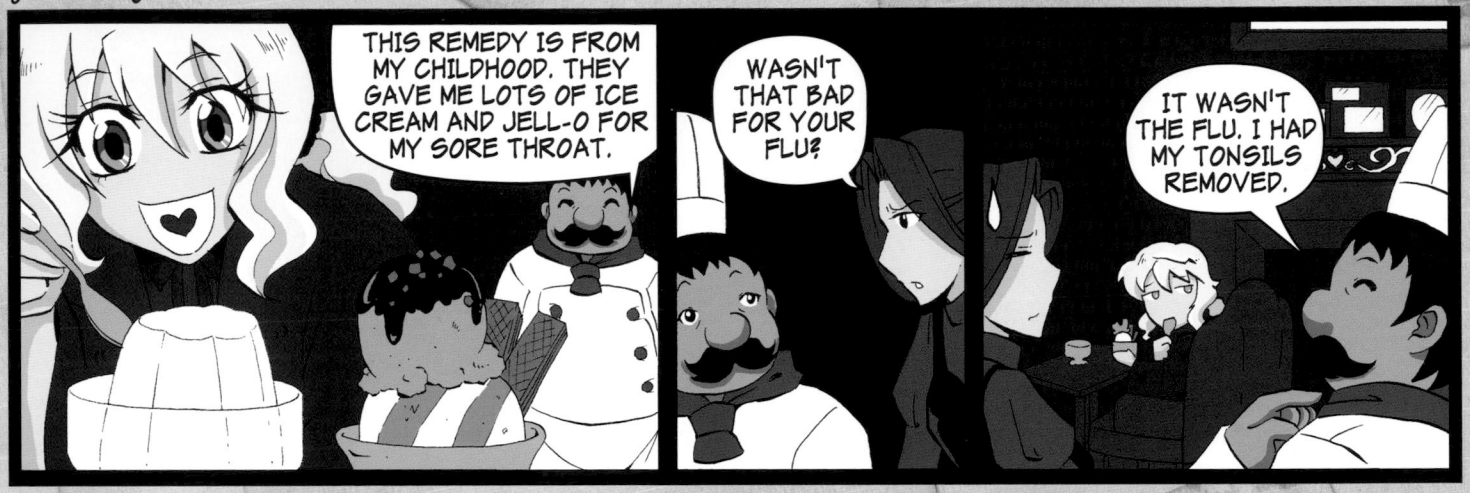

Sweet and Sour

dear diary

Even though being sick was a week of aches, pains and general misery, there's one thing that made it bearable--my friends and family. I didn't quite appreciate how much they really do care for me. I'm so lucky. I just hope that one day they'll somehow learn how much I care for them.

love forever

Ai

ARE YOU FEELING BETTER?
YEAH! EVEN MY SNIFFLE'S FINALLY STARTING TO CLEAR.
GUESS SAL'S HOME REMEDIES HELPED A LOT...
JELL-O
SOUP
BUTTERSCOTCH
MEDICINE
ICE CREAM
BUT NOT AS MUCH AS HAVING YOU GUYS PULLIN' FOR ME!
I HAVE ONE MORE REMEDY.
?
RING THIS--YOU'LL FEEL BETTER.
DING A LING
VISITING HOURS!

WE MADE YOU A GET-WELL CARD!
AND I DECLARED A NATIONAL HOLIDAY ON AI-LAND UNTIL YOU GET BETTER.
HOLIDAY? DADDY, I'M SICK, NOT DEAD!
WE LOVE YOU, PRINCESS AI!
Get Well Princess Ai
SNIFF-SNIFF
YOU'RE ALL SO SWEET! I LOVE YOU, TOO.

Diet

Rain, Rain

Lunchtime

Jammin'

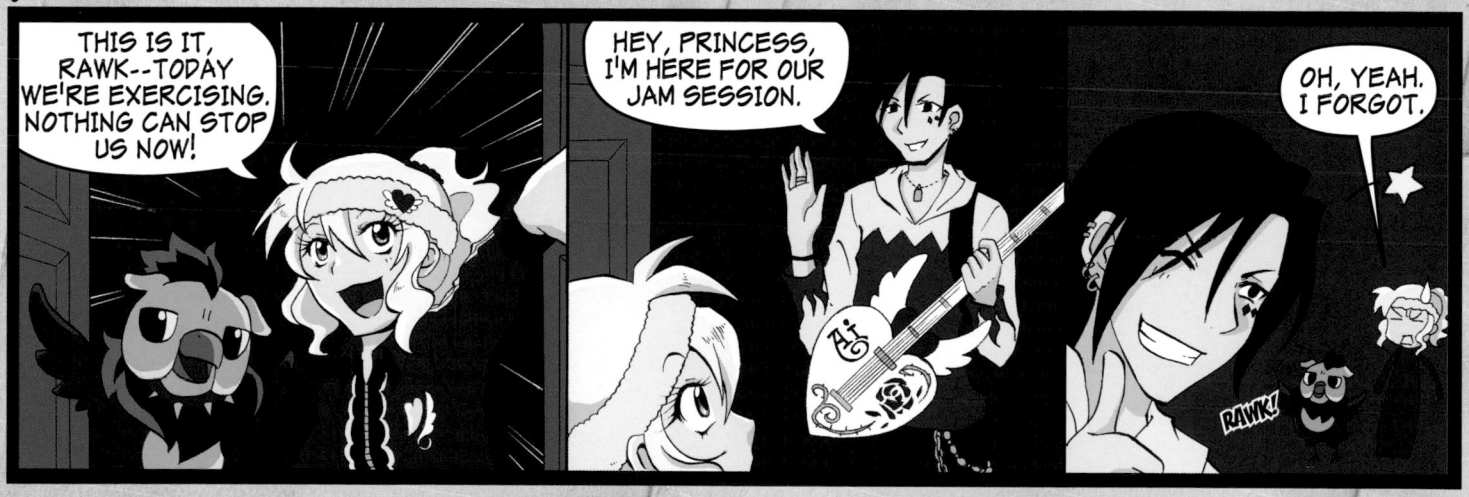

Day for Shopping

Eclipse

dear diary

I've been putting off exercise day after day. That's it--I'm finally gonna go to it! The key to getting motivated is wearing the right outfit. With stylish sweats and fresh kicks, I'm ready to lose some extra poundage! And doesn't little Rawk look simply adorable?

love forever

Ai

RAWK, TODAY'S THE DAY!
RAWK!
EXERCISE TIME!
NO RAIN...
NOW'S OUR CHANCE.
WHY DO PEOPLE RUN ANYWAY? HOW CAN IT BE GOOD WHEN YOU FEEL LIKE DYING?!!
Huff Huff
BESIDES, IT'S MUCH FASTER BY CAR.
RA... RA... RAWWW...

Dougen Slash Patrol
DSP

Die It

ANOTHER FINE MEAL FROM SAL.
MMMM.
CHOMP!
NO THANKS, SAL... THIS ONE LEAF WILL BE PLENTY.
NOW I KNOW WHY THEY CALL IT A "DIET."
'CAUSE IT FEELS LIKE I'M GONNA DIE!

Carbs

SAL, AI'S PLATE IS EMPTY.
I HAVE ALL I NEED FOR MY DIET RIGHT HERE.
? ? ?
I SEE NOTHING.
TODAY IS CARB-FREE BREAD DAY, DADDY... I'VE GOT TOASTED AIR.

Veggie Steak

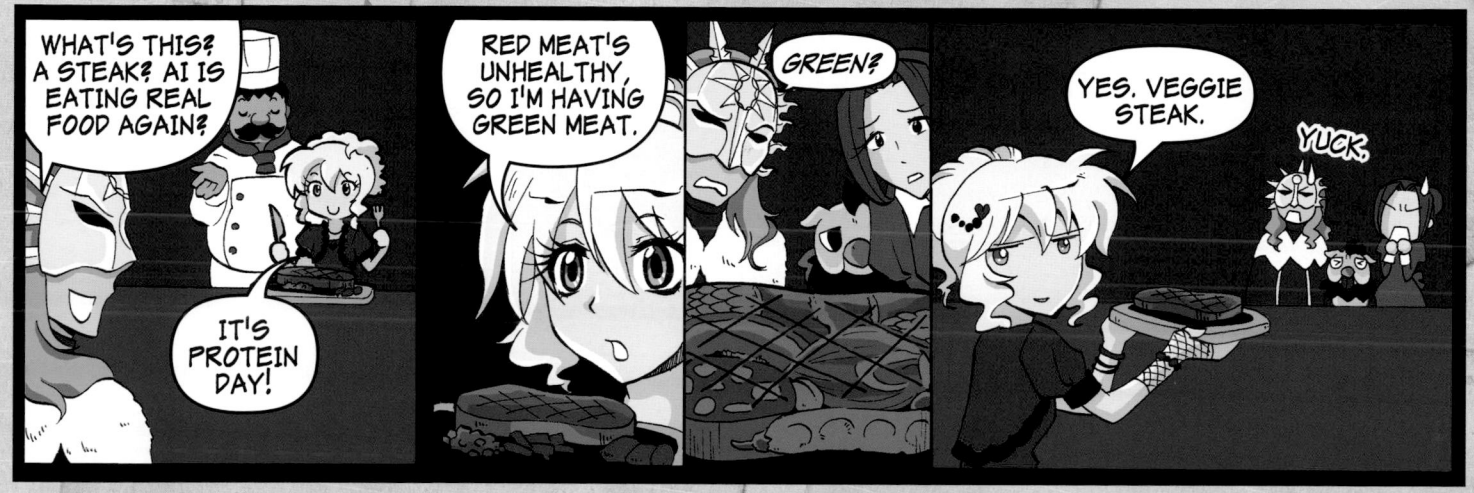

I See Cream

Chalkolate

Special Soup

dear diary

You know, it really stinks to be on a diet when you love food. When people talk about self-discipline, I think they really mean self-infliction--The pain! The pain! So why am I doing this to myself? I guess this means that I'm self-conscious and insecure. Lissa says I'm already skinny enough, but I only wanted to lose 10 extra pounds. Then would I be happy? I'm not so sure anymore. Maybe I just shouldn't worry about it and just try to be comfortable with who I am...

love forever

Ai

MMMMM
TWO MORE HOURS OF THE DIET TO GO...
YUM
Rawk!
AI'S ONE-WEEK CRASH DIET
OKAY, SCALE, GO EASY ON ME.
I LOST 10 POUNDS!
YOU MADE YOUR DIET GOAL!
OUR LONG NATIONAL ORDEAL IS OVER.
SO HOW SHOULD WE CELEBRATE?

YOU HAVE TO ASK? I'VE HAD ENOUGH WEIRD DIET FOOD TO LAST ME FOREVER.
PILE IT ON, SAL! I EARNED IT!
THAT WAS SO DELICIOUS! NOW LET ME JUST DOUBLE-CHECK MY WEIGHT...
+15 LBS.
NOOOOOOO!

Firewood

Jacques

Wood Chopping

Wood Carrying

Move Out of the Way

Ripped Shirt

dear diary

The Dougen...they're such a mystery. Who were they? It seems that everyone I know has a different opinion. After all, they're practically extinct. Besides Rawk and Daddy's unicorns, I've never even seen them. Some people say they looked like terrible beasts; others say they were angels. Then there was the war. They tried to destroy us--but Daddy drove them off. Will I ever find out their secrets?

love forever

Ai

ANOTHER PILE OF WOOD CHOPPED AND NEATLY STACKED.
LADIES! INTERESTED IN HEARING AN OLD LUMBERJACK STORY?
OH, JACQUES! YOU'RE SO STRONG AND HANDSOME!
YEAH!
I'LL TALK QUIETLY SO THE KING DOESN'T CATCH ME TAKING A BREAK.
IN THE BEGINNING OF AI-LAND, THE DOUGEN WERE WILDER, FIERCER.
BUT EVEN THE DOUGEN WERE AFRAID OF THE GIANT WOOD MONSTER.

WHEREVER THE GIANT WOOD MONSTER ROAMED, DESTRUCTION SURELY FOLLOWED.
ONE FOGGY MORNING, THE FOREST DOUGEN FOUND HIM COLLAPSED ON THE GROUND.
RAWK!
DADDY!
THAT'S IT, YOUNG MAN!
...UNLESS YOU TELL ME WHAT HAPPENED TO THE GIANT WOOD MONSTER!
YOU ARE IN ENORMOUS TROUBLE...

Tired

Got One

Big One

IT'S GONNA BE A BIG ONE!
HERE IT COMES! IT FEELS HUGE!
YEAH, HUGE.

Bait

HOW MANY YOU GUYS GOT?
TWO.
ONE...
14!
YOU CAN'T COUNT THE BAIT.

Rawk Lobster

Gum not Fish

dear diary

Lissa calls my singing magical. I'm not so sure about that, but I definitely feel some sort of magic inside with music. It's almost like my entire body wants to float through the air like musical notes. I don't know why, but it seems like music is its own language, and I'm still learning how to speak it. Maybe no one can quite understand--even I don't get it entirely. I just know that music is something I couldn't live without.

love forever

Ai

GOODNESS, IT'S COLD.
WINTER IS THE BEST TIME TO CATCH FISH. THEIR FAT CONTENT IS AT ITS HIGHEST.
PRINCESS, ANY BITES YET?
NO. NOTHING AT ALL.
I'VE GOT AN IDEA!

Dougen Slash Patrol DSP

Arbor Day

White Christmas

Stockings

Reindeer

Presents

X-mas Carols

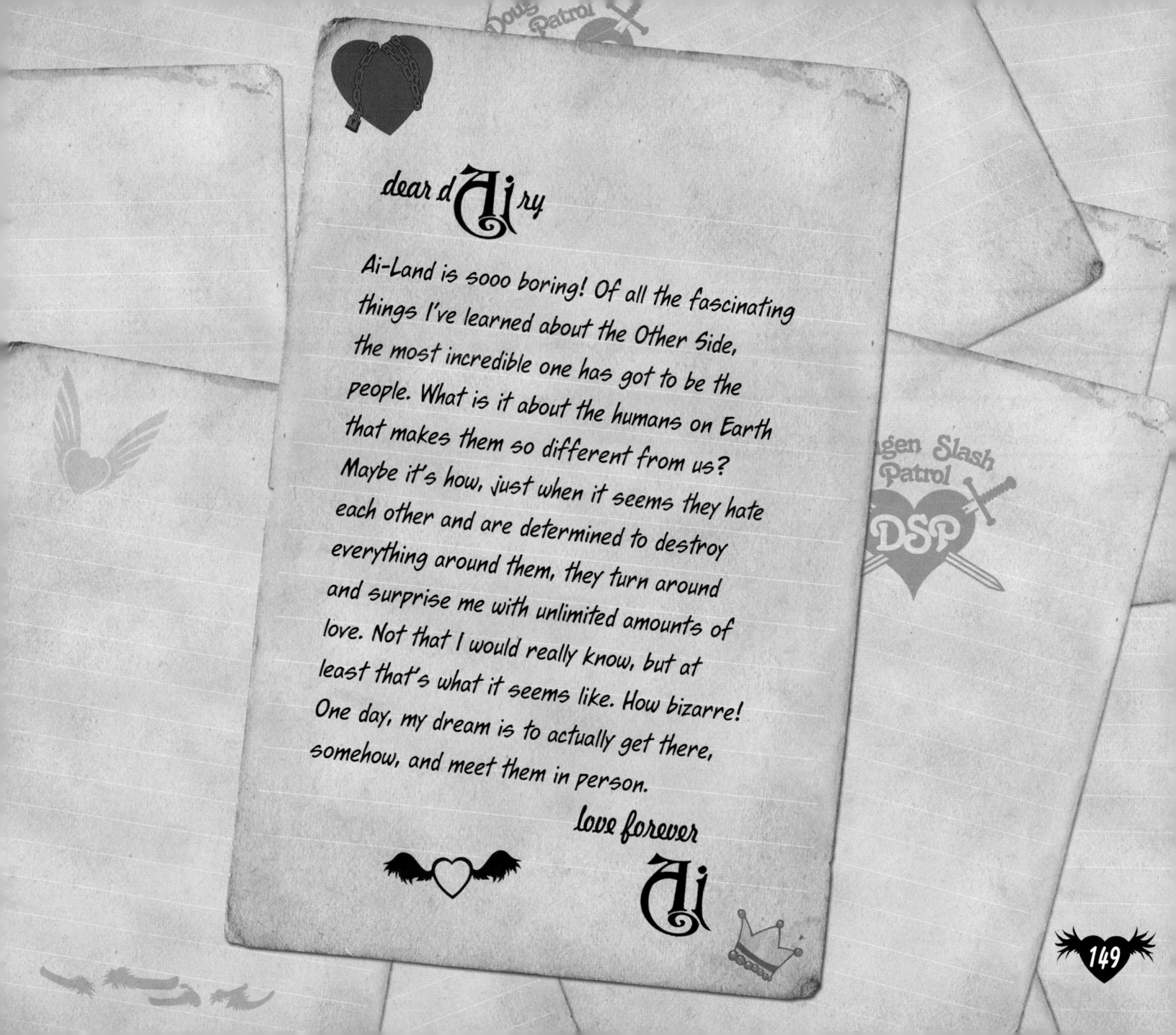

dear dAiry

Ai-Land is sooo boring! Of all the fascinating things I've learned about the Other Side, the most incredible one has got to be the people. What is it about the humans on Earth that makes them so different from us? Maybe it's how, just when it seems they hate each other and are determined to destroy everything around them, they turn around and surprise me with unlimited amounts of love. Not that I would really know, but at least that's what it seems like. How bizarre! One day, my dream is to actually get there, somehow, and meet them in person.

love forever

Ai

OH, PRINCESS! I CAN'T BELIEVE IT-- CHRISTMAS, HERE ON AI-LAND.
AND HERE'S THE FINAL TOUCH!
SNOW? HERE ON AI-LAND?!
THANKS, JACQUES.
HEY, GUYS, C'MON IN!

DADDY, THIS PRESENT IS FOR YOU.
THIS CHRISTMAS THING--IT SEEMS TOO GOOD TO BE TRUE. WHAT'S THE SECRET TO ITS MAGIC?
IT'S THE LOVE OF FAMILY AND FRIENDS THAT MAKES CHRISTMAS A MAGICAL TIME.
MERRY CHRISTMAS!!
LOVE
THAT'S IT!
I HEREBY PROCLAIM CHRISTMAS AN AI-LAND HOLIDAY FROM THIS YEAR FORTH!
YAAAAY!

Resolution # 1: No Diet

Resolution # 2: Shop 'Til You Drop

Resolution # 3: Blisters on Fingers

Resolution # 4: Find Lissa a Boyfriend

Resolution # 5: Activist

Resolution # 6: Dreadful Wings

dear dAiry

It's New Year's Eve here on Ai-Land, just like it is on the Other Side--Earth. Everyone's making resolutions to change. That's so weird. Every time I try to change, things never turn out like I planned. Like when I try to lose weight. But sometimes, I wake up, and I've just--changed. I guess that's what growing up is all about. It doesn't always make sense, especially to Daddy. But that's the way it is for me, here on Ai-Land.

love forever

Ai

JAN
IT'S OFFICIAL...
ANOTHER YEAR DONE.
PRINCESS, DID YOU FINISH YOUR NEW YEAR'S RESOLUTIONS?
OF COURSE.
I'VE COME UP WITH RESOLUTIONS THAT WILL HELP ALL OF YOU IMPROVE YOURSELVES IN THE NEW YEAR.
HERE!
WOW! THAT'S SOME LIST.

Dougen Slash Patrol DSP

TOKYOPOP®

AVAILABLE NOW

PRINCESS AI: THE MANGA TRILOGY

Princess Ai tries to piece together clues about how she ended up on Earth, as the forces of love and chaos close in around her...

PRINCESS AI: RUMORS FROM THE OTHER SIDE

Who would dare print rumors, innuendo and bald-faced lies about everyone's favorite international rock diva Princess Ai?

PRINCESS AI: THE ULTIMATE EDITION

All volumes in the manga trilogy are collected here, with never-before-seen bonus material.

PRINCESS AI: ROSES & TATTOOS

This limited edition full-color book features new art and poetry by the Princess Ai creators.

EXPLORE THE WORLD OF

Princess Ai

The manga was just the beginning! There's so much going on in the world of Princess Ai—and so much more to come. Here's a peek at the past, present, and future of Ai Land.

AVAILABLE WHEREVER BOOKS ARE SOLD.
OR VISIT WWW.TOKYOPOP.COM/SHOP
KEYWORD: "PRINCESS AI"

COMING SOON

Stay tuned to www.TOKYOPOP.com for more information!

PRINCESS AI HITS THE BIG SCREEN

This groundbreaking feature film is a Gothic Rock Opera! The Japan-U.S. co-production is a stunning blend of live action and anime.

PRINCESS AI: AI-TUNES

The long-awaited soundtrack to the original manga trilogy.

PRINCESS AI: THE PRISM OF MIDNIGHT DAWN

The stunning new manga sequel! In this new trilogy, Princess Ai ventures to the Other Side to retrieve the stolen Prism of Midnight Dawn...

PRINCESS AI BROKEN LEASH

The sizzling music video for "Broken Leash"—from the collection of music videos being produced by the creative team behind the upcoming feature film.

PRINCESS AI: ENCOUNTERS

A collection of stories following Ai as she journeys across the TOKYOPOP Universe—and into bestselling manga series.

TOKYOPOP®

Princess Ai of Ai-Land: The Comic Strip Collection

Written by Stu "Milky" Levy

Illustrated by Pauro Izaki

Princess Ai Created by Courtney Love and Stu "Milky" Levy

Lettering - Jennifer Carbajal, Chelsea Windlinger, and Fawn Lau
Cover Design - Jennifer Carbajal
Cover Art - Pauro Izaki
Color and Tones - Mara Aum

Editors - Rie Shiramizu and Jeremy Ross
Digital Imaging Manager - Chris Buford
Pre-Production Supervisor - Lucas Rivera
Production Manager - Elisabeth Brizzi
Managing Editor - Vy Nguyen
Creative Director - Anne Marie Horne
Editor-in-Chief - Rob Tokar
Publisher - Mike Kiley
President and C.O.O. - John Parker
C.E.O. and Chief Creative Officer - Stu Levy

A TOKYOPOP® Manga

TOKYOPOP and are trademarks or registered trademarks of TOKYOPOP Inc.

TOKYOPOP Inc.
5900 Wilshire Blvd. Suite 2000
Los Angeles, CA 90036

E-mail: info@TOKYOPOP.com
Come visit us online at www.TOKYOPOP.com

The author and editors would like to give their appreciation for the wonderful people at Andrews McMeel Universal who syndicated *Princess Ai of Ai-Land* in newspapers. Special thanks to John Glynn, Cathy Kirkland, Lucas Wetzel, Patty Adams, Chris Craver, Robert Hightower and the rest of the AMU team.

© 2008 TOKYOPOP Inc. and Kitty Radio, Inc. All Rights Reserved. Princess Ai and Ai of Ai-Land are trademarks of TOKYOPOP Inc. and Kitty Radio, Inc.

All rights reserved. No portion of this book may be reproduced or transmitted in any form or by any means without written permission from the copyright holders. This manga is a work of fiction. Any resemblance to actual events or locales or persons, living or dead, is entirely coincidental.

ISBN: 978-1-4278-1163-9

First TOKYOPOP printing: July 2008

10 9 8 7 6 5 4 3 2 1

Printed in China